BACK LANE WINERIES *of* NAPA

BACK LANE WINERIES

OF

NAPA

Second Edition

TILAR MAZZEO
PHOTOGRAPHY BY PAUL HAWLEY

TEN SPEED PRESS
Berkeley

Previous edition originally published in the United States by The Little
Bookroom, New York, in 2010.
All photographs by Paul Hawley with the exception of the following:
Page 86: Olabisi Winery
Page 99: Tara Katrina Hole
Page 110: Cimarossa
Page 117: Ladera Vineyards
Page 141: Robert Keenan Winery
Page 182, 184: Ehlers Estate
Page 186, 187: Rutherford Grove
Page 197: Keever Vineyards

Library of Congress Cataloging-in-Publication Data
Mazzeo, Tilar J.
  The back lane wineries of Napa / Tilar J. Mazzeo ; photographs by Paul
Hawley. – Second edition.
    pages cm
Includes index.
  1. Wine tourism—California—Napa Valley. 2. Wine tasting—California—
Napa Valley. 3. Wineries—California—Napa Valley—Guidebooks. 4. Napa
Valley (Calif.)—Guidebooks. I. Title.
  TP548.5.T68M38 2014
  663'.20979419—dc23
                                    2013031995

Trade Paperback ISBN: 978-1-60774-590-7
eBook ISBN: 978-1-60774-591-4

Printed in China

Design by Katy Brown
Cartography by Moon Street Cartography, Durango, Colorado

10 9 8 7 6 5 4 3 2 1

Second Edition

Contents

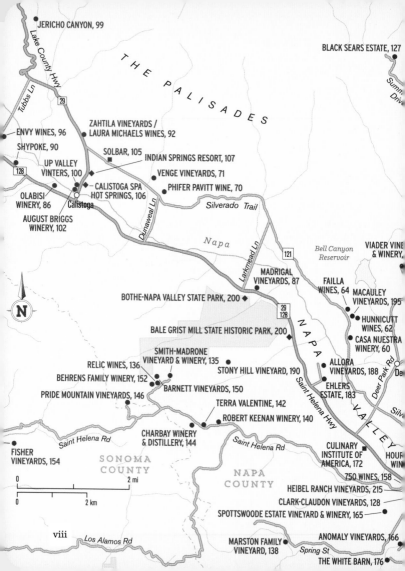

JERICHO CANYON, 99

BLACK SEARS ESTATE, 127

Summi
Driv

THE PALISADES

Lake County Hwy

Tubbs Ln

29

ENVY WINES, 96

ZAHTILA VINEYARDS /
LAURA MICHAELS WINES, 92

SHYPOKE, 90

SOLBAR, 105

INDIAN SPRINGS RESORT, 107

128

UP VALLEY
VINTERS, 100

VENGE VINEYARDS, 71

CALISTOGA SPA
HOT SPRINGS, 106

PHIFER PAVITT WINE, 70

OLABISI
WINERY, 86

Calistoga

Silverado Trail

AUGUST BRIGGS
WINERY, 102

Dunaweal Ln

Napa

121

Bell Canyon
Reservoir

VIADER VINE
& WINERY,

Larkmead Ln

MADRIGAL
VINEYARDS, 87

FAILLA
WINES, 64

MACAULEY
VINEYARDS, 195

N

BOTHE-NAPA VALLEY STATE PARK, 200

29
128

HUNNICUTT
WINES, 62

NAPA

CASA NUESTRA
WINERY, 60

BALE GRIST MILL STATE HISTORIC PARK, 200

SMITH-MADRONE
VINEYARD & WINERY, 135

ALLORA
VINEYARDS, 188

De

RELIC WINES, 136

STONY HILL VINEYARD, 190

Deer Park Rd

BEHRENS FAMILY WINERY, 152

Saint Helena Hwy

EHLERS
ESTATE, 183

BARNETT VINEYARDS, 150

PRIDE MOUNTAIN VINEYARDS, 146

TERRA VALENTINE, 142

VALLEY

ROBERT KEENAN WINERY, 140

Silv

FISHER
VINEYARDS, 154

Saint Helena Rd

CHARBAY WINERY
& DISTILLERY, 144

Saint Helena Rd

CULINARY
INSTITUTE OF
AMERICA, 172

HOUR
WIN

SONOMA
COUNTY

NAPA
COUNTY

750 WINES, 158

0   2 mi

HEIBEL RANCH VINEYARDS, 215

0   2 km

CLARK-CLAUDON VINEYARDS, 128

SPOTTSWOODE ESTATE VINEYARD & WINERY, 165

viii

ANOMALY VINEYARDS, 166

Los Alamos Rd

MARSTON FAMILY
VINEYARD, 138

Spring St

THE WHITE BARN, 176

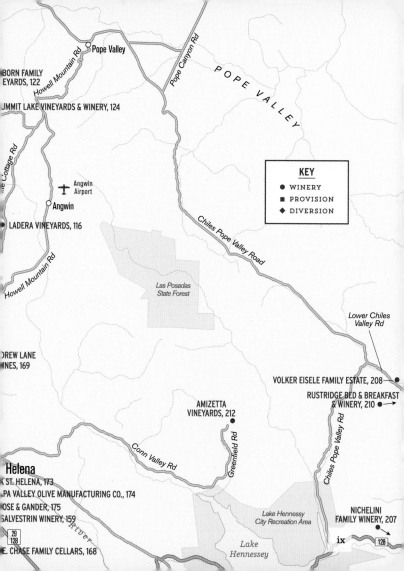

KEY
● WINERY
■ PROVISION
◆ DIVERSION

POPE VALLEY

Pope Valley

Pope Canyon Rd

Howell Mountain Rd

BORN FAMILY
EYARDS, 122

UMMIT LAKE VINEYARDS & WINERY, 124

e Cottage Rd

Angwin Airport

Angwin

LADERA VINEYARDS, 116

Howell Mountain Rd

Chiles Pope Valley Road

Las Posadas
State Forest

Lower Chiles
Valley Rd

DREW LANE
NES, 169

VOLKER EISELE FAMILY ESTATE, 208 ●

RUSTRIDGE BED & BREAKFAST
& WINERY, 210 ●→

AMIZETTA
VINEYARDS, 212 ●

Conn Valley Rd

Greenfield Rd

Chiles Pope Valley Rd

Helena

K ST. HELENA, 173

PA VALLEY OLIVE MANUFACTURING CO., 174

OSE & GANDER, 175

SALVESTRIN WINERY, 159

River

Lake Hennessy
City Recreation Area

NICHELINI
FAMILY WINERY, 207
●

29
128

E. CHASE FAMILY CELLARS, 168

Lake
Hennessy

ix

128

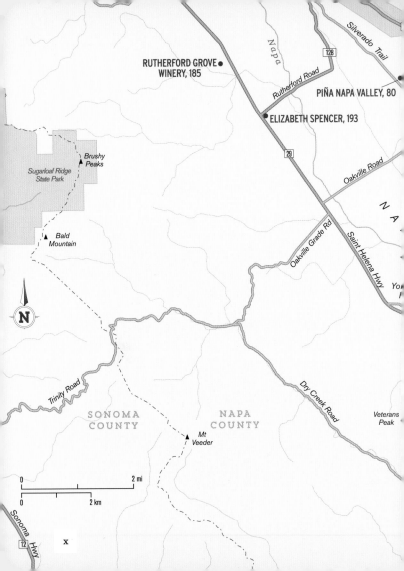

RUTHERFORD GROVE WINERY, 185

PIÑA NAPA VALLEY, 80

ELIZABETH SPENCER, 193

Brushy Peaks

Sugarloaf Ridge State Park

Bald Mountain

Napa

128

Rutherford Road

Silverado Trail

Oakville Road

29

Oakville Grade Rd

Saint Helena Hwy

Trinity Road

N A

Yo

Dry Creek Road

Veterans Peak

SONOMA COUNTY

NAPA COUNTY

Mt Veeder

0   2 mi

0   2 km

Sonoma Hwy

12

x

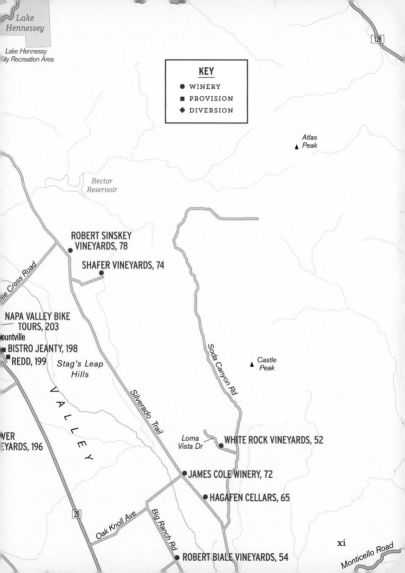

KEY

- ● WINERY
- ■ PROVISION
- ◆ DIVERSION

Lake Hennessey

Lake Hennessy City Recreation Area

128

▲ Atlas Peak

Rector Reservoir

● ROBERT SINSKEY VINEYARDS, 78

● SHAFER VINEYARDS, 74

le Cross Road

■ NAPA VALLEY BIKE TOURS, 203

ountville

■ BISTRO JEANTY, 198

■ REDD, 199

Stag's Leap Hills

▲ Castle Peak

Soda Canyon Rd

Silverado Trail

V A L L E Y

VER EYARDS, 196

Loma Vista Dr

● WHITE ROCK VINEYARDS, 52

● JAMES COLE WINERY, 72

● HAGAFEN CELLARS, 65

29

Oak Knoll Ave

Big Ranch Rd

● ROBERT BIALE VINEYARDS, 54

xi

Monticello Road

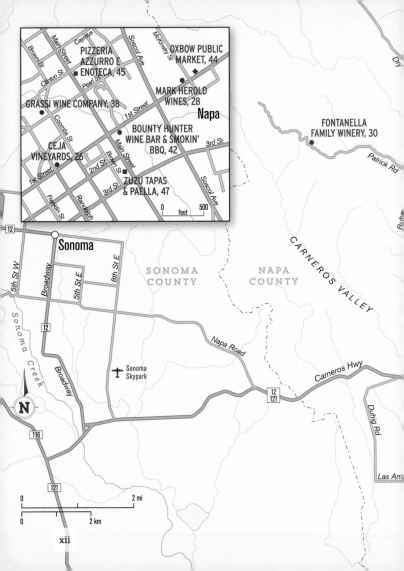

PIZZERIA AZZURRO E ENOTECA, 45

OXBOW PUBLIC MARKET, 44

MARK HEROLD WINES, 28

Napa

GRASSI WINE COMPANY, 38

BOUNTY HUNTER WINE BAR & SMOKIN' BBQ, 42

CEJA VINEYARDS, 26

ZUZU TAPAS & PAELLA, 47

Main Street

Caymus

Main Street

Brown St

Clinton St

Pearl St

Coombs St

1st Street

Ceja Vineyards

Franklin St

Randolph

Brown St

1st Street

2nd St

3rd St

Soscol Ave

McKinstry St

3rd St

3rd St

Soscol Ave

FONTANELLA FAMILY WINERY, 30

Patrick Rd

Dry

Rutz

0   feet   500

Sonoma

5th St W

Broadway

5th St E

8th St E

12

SONOMA COUNTY

NAPA COUNTY

CARNEROS VALLEY

Napa Road

Sonoma Skypark

Carneros Hwy

12 121

Duhig Rd

Sonoma Creek

Broadway

N

116

121

0   2 mi

0   2 km

Las Am

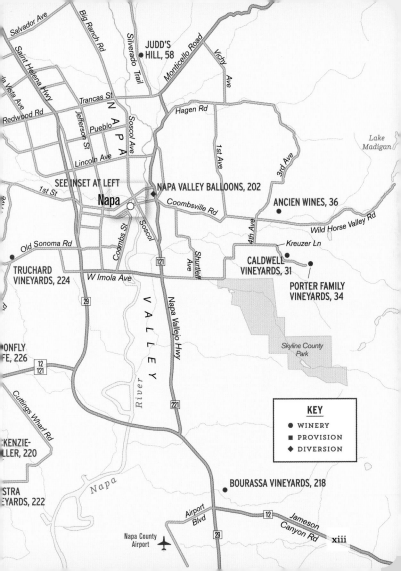

JUDD'S HILL, 58

NAPA VALLEY BALLOONS, 202

ANCIEN WINES, 36

SEE INSET AT LEFT

Napa

Coombsville Rd

Wild Horse Valley Rd

Kreuzer Ln

CALDWELL VINEYARDS, 31

PORTER FAMILY VINEYARDS, 34

Old Sonoma Rd

TRUCHARD VINEYARDS, 224

W Imola Ave

Skyline County Park

ONFLY FE, 226

KENZIE-LLER, 220

STRA EYARDS, 222

BOURASSA VINEYARDS, 218

Airport Blvd

Napa County Airport

Jameson Canyon Rd

KEY

● WINERY

■ PROVISION

◆ DIVERSION

Salvador Ave

Big Ranch Rd

Silverado Trail

Monticello Road

Vichy Ave

Saint Helena Hwy

la Vista Ave

Redwood Rd

Trancas St

Hagen Rd

Jefferson St

Pueblo

Soscol Ave

1st Ave

3rd Ave

Lincoln Ave

N A P A

Lake Madigan

1st St

Coombs St

Soscol

Shurtleff Ave

4th Ave

Coombs St

V A L L E Y

Napa Vallejo Hwy

Napa River

Cuttings Wharf Rd

Napa

xiii

Introduction

THE REPUTATION OF THE NAPA VALLEY is the stuff of legend, and the making of the California wine country is a story with enough drama and intrigue to support more than a handful of bestselling accounts of its rise to international prominence. Since the famous face-off in the 1976 so-called "Judgment of Paris"—where Napa Valley Chardonnay and Cabernet Sauvignon wines beat out renowned French competitors in blind tests—there has been no doubt that this relatively small corner of the wine world has garnered a big reputation. Consider, after all, that the Napa Valley produces less than five percent of the total wine production in the state of California. Or that it has fewer than fifty thousand acres planted to vineyards. Bordeaux has more than five times that amount, and, yet, devoted aficionados of Napa Valley wines will argue that their reputations are not all that different.

The result of all this celebrity and acclaim is more than just great wines. It also means tourism. Each year, nearly five million visitors travel to the Napa Valley wine country from around the world. Most of these visitors travel along what the locals call "the loop"—the well-trodden tasting route that takes eager enthusiasts up the Silverado Trail and back down the St. Helena Highway (or vice versa), past some of America's most famous and most familiar wineries. Along the way, there are picturesque fields of blazing mustard blooms, ready gourmet pleasures, and a little taste of the good life, Napa style.

If what you want is a weekend (or more) of incomparable luxury, you'll have no trouble finding it here in the wine country, and you won't need a travel guide if what you want to do is visit the celebrated commercial wineries of the Napa Valley. It's hard to miss them. Many tasting rooms are slick retail operations run by corporate managers living somewhere a long way from Napa, offering wines that you can buy just as readily (and often less expensively) on the shelves of your local grocery store, and big signs along the highway will show you the way. Often, these are beautiful places, and I am not recommending that you pass them by entirely. A part of the California wine tasting experience is sitting on marbled Italianate terraces overlooking acres of perfectly pruned vineyards, basking in the warm sun and the intense loveliness of it all.

For some, as exquisite as it all is, there is also a whispered complaint. To certain sensibilities, it's just possible that this aspect of Napa is a bit more like Disneyland than anyone would like. The largest corporate wineries crank out more than eight million cases of wine a year, and the hillsides are dotted with mansions that you can tell even from a distance are monstrously huge. It's all too easy to get the impression that Napa is big business by day and elite charity events by night—the kind of place where the idle super-rich, weighed down by all those diamonds, struggle to lift that $100 glass of hillside cabernet. And sometimes there is the perception that only heaven can help the poor novice who wanders off the beaten tourist track. At least there on the main tourist trail, lost in a crowd, you can slink away silently when the experts start in on some competitive and very expensive appreciation.

These are some of the enduring stereotypes of Napa—maybe even part of the marketing in some corners of the valley. But nothing could be farther from the heart and soul of this region. The other side of the wine country, and by far the larger side, is surprisingly genuine, low-key, and embracing, a place where enthusiastic amateurs are everyone's favorite people and where you can spend a long afternoon tromping the vineyards with a small proprietor who is only too happy to share with you his or her little piece of paradise for a remarkably modest tasting fee—and sometimes without charging at all. Out there in the fields or up in the tasting room, you'll hear time and time again the story of how one winemaker or another came to this verdant valley, fell in love with it, and found the course of life irrevocably altered. Everywhere in Napa there are people of passion who have made their life's work crafting a beautiful wine.

Here in the wine country, there are also more than a few families who have farmed these ranches for decades and can still remember a time when most of this valley was planted not to grapes but to fruit orchards. These are folks with deep community ties and pioneering histories—and part of what they helped pioneer was that special way of life in the wine country that still has the power to enchant so many of those who come to visit.

It's only along the back lanes that you'll get to hear those kinds of stories, and, because many of these wines aren't widely distributed, it's also only along the back lanes that you'll get a chance to try them. They are, as often as not, world-class wines that locals and industry insiders revere but that few consumers will ever encounter in a wine shop. Without the pressures of large-scale commercialization, these are also the cellars where old varietals can be preserved or new experiments in shaping the future of enology can be put to the test.

These small outfits won't have big advertising budgets or well-posted tasting rooms along the major thoroughfares—and they don't want them either. So the trouble for a newcomer to the Napa Valley is where to start looking. This is a guide to those back lane wineries of Napa, places where you can find excellent handcrafted wines made by on-site proprietors, often with only a local or regional distribution and with a limited case production. With only a handful of exceptions, the wineries included in this book make fewer than ten thousand cases of wine a year, and the smallest produce only a hundred or so. Those larger exceptions are wineries that are so much a part of the heart and soul of Napa's history that I couldn't bear to exclude them, and their case productions still number only in the tens of thousands. In a county where some of the big commercial operations churn out millions of cases of wine a year, this is still a small operation.

Off the beaten path there are few marble terraces or stucco palaces, but often these wineries are in the midst of striking beauty—overlooking a hundred acres of a wildlife preserve far above the fog-lined valley floor, on the edge of an ancient redwood forest, or tucked along a rural side road in the middle of open fields, where the proprietors are happy to watch you settle down for a picnic with a bottle or two of wine.

Best of all, in my mind, these are places where wine tasting gets down to earth. Here, no one needs to show off how developed his or her palate is, and the winemakers welcome questions from beginners and experts alike. Above all, these are wines that are likely to be a new experience, with names that you won't find in big retail outlets back home. Amid the back lane wineries of Napa, you can still make secret discoveries.

How to Use This Book

THE NAPA VALLEY WINE-GROWING REGION, one of the world's most recognizable appellations in its own right, encompasses more than a dozen subappellations (currently sixteen), each with a particular microclimate and with particular grape varietals that thrive in the region, and often the wines are remarkably distinct. Visitors are frequently surprised to discover that a relatively small area can produce wines of such diversity.

This diversity is the result of the area's geological history, which has created a long, narrow valley running some thirty-odd miles between two steep mountain ranges along the ancient contours of the Napa River, from San Pablo Bay in the south to as far north as Calistoga, at the foot of Mount St. Helena. The Vacas Mountains rise up above the valley floor to the east, and they are home to some of the region's most famous hillside vineyards, including the celebrated Howell Mountain subappellation. To the west are the Mayacamas, which divide Napa County from Sonoma County, and where highly regarded new vineyards are being developed.

Two main roads run the length of the valley floor. On the western side of the valley is Highway 29, which is also known as the St. Helena Highway, and this is the region's main tasting route. It takes visitors through the area's small towns, where you will find restaurants, hotels, and, of course, tasting rooms. On the eastern side of the valley is Highway 121, which, when it runs through the wine country, is known as the Silverado Trail—or to locals as "the trail"—a more rural and scenic road that passes acres of vineyards and is dotted with dozens of premium wineries. Directions are given from one or both of these routes, and your best bet for navigating the region is to pick up one of the free maps available at almost any tasting room or hotel.

If Highway 29 and the Silverado Trail may be said to run roughly parallel to each other, then you'll also want to know that they are connected at various points by a series of crossroads, which begin with Trancas Street to the south (in the town of Napa) and progress northward at Oak Knoll Avenue, Yountville Cross Road, Oakville Cross Road, Highway 128 at Rutherford Road, Zinfandel Lane, Deer Park Road, Lodi Lane, Bale Lane, Larkmead Lane, and Highway 29 at Lincoln Avenue (in the town of Calistoga). Those are your best bets for getting from one side of the valley to the other, and, though the locals won't thank me for mentioning it, it's handy to know that, when the traffic on the St. Helena Highway is too hopelessly congested to bear, things are often much quicker just a bit to the east.

Although the region is world famous for its wines, much of the valley remains uncultivated, and, as a result, the Napa Valley American Viticultural Area—or AVA—is spread out over a relatively large area. Because it can easily take more than an hour of steady driving to get across the region, the best way to plan a day of wine tasting is to focus on a couple of subappellations, taking time for a leisurely gourmet lunch and some sightseeing along the way. If you are visiting up in the mountains or in the eastern valleys, keep in mind that the only dependable options for either gasoline or lunch are in Napa or along the St. Helena Highway.

To understand AVA classifications in the Napa Valley, it's important to remember that Napa Valley is its own AVA. Within that larger wine-growing region there are also more than a dozen distinct subappellations, areas characterized by unique growing conditions and microclimates, including Howell Mountain, Chiles Valley District, Atlas Peak, Spring Mountain District, Mount Veeder, Los Carneros, Oak Knoll District of Napa Valley, Stag's Leap, Coombsville, Yountville, Oakville, Wild Horse Valley, Rutherford, St. Helena, Diamond Mountain, and Calistoga. Some of the smaller and more remote areas—places like Atlas Peak, Wild Horse Valley, Mount Veeder, and Diamond Mountain District AVA—have very limited opportunities for visits, and many of the wineries in these areas maintain tasting rooms down on the valley floor. For this reason, these wineries can be found mixed in among the different sections of this book. While understanding the nuances of appellations is important to appreciating the wines from the Napa Valley, this guide is arranged loosely by route rather than strictly by classification, with an eye toward helping you plan a convenient tasting itinerary that might take in a couple of different wine-growing areas. It's a chance in the course of a day (or more) to experience just how different one growing region can be from the next—even when the distance is only a matter of miles or minutes. At the end of each section are suggestions for nearby restaurants or local attractions that you can work in spontaneously.

The book is divided into nine different tasting areas:

DOWNTOWN NAPA AND ENVIRONS (Chapter 1; shown on maps on pages xii–xiii) includes wineries and tasting rooms conveniently clustered around the city of Napa, where you'll also find outdoor markets, some of the valley's best evening entertainment, and good casual dining options. This section also includes wineries and tasting rooms in the valley's newest AVA, Coombsville, a region to the east of Napa with a long history, rolling benchland vineyards, and close proximity to San Francisco.

SILVERADO TRAIL (Chapter 2; shown on maps on pages x–xi and xii–xiii) covers wineries along this famous tasting route on the eastern side of the Napa Valley and includes the acclaimed Stag's Leap and Oak Knoll districts.

CALISTOGA AND ENVIRONS (Chapter 3; shown on maps on pages viii–ix) includes the tasting rooms conveniently clustered along the north end of the Silverado Trail and the St. Helena Highway within easy striking distance of the city of Calistoga, renowned for its mineral baths and home to some excellent casual dining opportunities.

HOWELL MOUNTAIN (Chapter 4; shown on maps on pages viii–ix) takes in the sometimes remote and always lovely Howell Mountain wineries that are located in the foothills on the eastern side of the Napa Valley.

SPRING MOUNTAIN (Chapter 5; shown on maps on pages viii–ix) takes in the equally remote and beautiful mountain wineries that are located in the foothills on the western side of the Napa Valley.

DOWNTOWN ST. HELENA AND ENVIRONS (Chapter 6; shown on maps on pages viii–ix) covers wineries in the area immediately surrounding the picturesque town of St. Helena, home to some of the region's most charming small shops and mouthwatering bistros. This section includes wineries that are producing primarily in the St. Helena AVA.

ST. HELENA HIGHWAY (Chapter 7; shown on maps on pages viii–ix and x–xi) encompasses the small family tasting rooms tucked among the commercial giants along Highway 29 and includes tasting room options in the Rutherford, Oakville, and Yountville AVAs. Wine aficionados will know that the town of Yountville is also deservedly famous for its world-class dining options.

EASTERN VALLEYS (Chapter 8; shown on maps on pages viii–ix) covers the smaller and more remote valleys tucked into the eastern foothills of the Napa Valley, including the Chiles Valley District and Pope Valley AVAs.

LOS CARNEROS AND ENVIRONS SOUTH OF NAPA (Chapter 9; shown on maps on pages xii–xiii) includes the cooler-climate growing region of the Carneros AVA, which Napa County shares with its neighboring Sonoma County, and some of the off-the-beaten-path wineries located south of the city of Napa.

Within all sections, you can also find wines produced within the more general—and immediately recognizable—Napa Valley AVA.

All the wineries listed in this book are open to visitors in some capacity, with just one or two notable exceptions too good to pass up, and wine tasting hours throughout the county are generally from 10 a.m. to 4:30 p.m. daily, although some wineries have longer or shorter hours, and it is always a good idea to call ahead to confirm opening times, especially early in the week (Monday and Tuesday particularly). Groups larger than six people should always call ahead to be sure the winemakers can accommodate them.

Many of the best small wineries are open by appointment only. You should not feel in the least bit shy about making the call. If a winemaker requires advance notice, it just means that he or she wants to be sure the tasting room is staffed that afternoon, and it is usually a sign that the person behind the bar will be the same person who goes out pruning the vines other days of the week. Often these winemaker tours are exceptional educational experiences and a rare opportunity to get an inside perspective on the craft of winemaking. Generally, it's a good idea to call at least a week in advance to set up appointments, and, in the busy summer months, appointments several weeks in advance are strongly recommended. Should you find yourself in the wine country unexpectedly, however, there's absolutely no harm in making a spur-of-the-moment call. Often, the winemakers are able to welcome even last-minute visitors.

Due to local zoning legislation and efforts to preserve the rural agricultural charm of the area, the trend is moving very strongly in the direction of "by appointment only." Keep in mind that if you just turn up at a tasting room zoned for visits "by appointment only," the winemaker will have to turn you away. The penalties from the governing bodies that regulate the wine industry are just too severe and can run to fines in the six figures, rumor has it. A call from your cell phone over lunch to make an appointment that same day is fair game, and, while the winemaker might very well not be able to accommodate you, no one will be in the least offended by your interest.

When you are planning your trip, keep in mind that weekends are the busiest time for wine tasting, especially at the commercial wineries, and in the summer months you will often have to jostle for a place at the tasting bar. A busy Saturday is the perfect time to head off the beaten path and visit some of the back lane wineries. Locals prefer to go wine tasting on Thursday and Friday mornings, when most places are open and gearing up for the weekend. If you are planning to visit in September, plan with particular care: the harvest—known in the California wine country as "the crush"—takes place around then, and the tasting room hours can be limited, but there are often opportunities to participate in other special events and harvest suppers during what can be one of the most festive times of the winemaking year.

And what will all this cost? Many tasting rooms (and nearly all the commercial ones) charge modest tasting fees, ranging from $10 to $15 for a "flight" of wines—a small taste of several different wines. It generally costs a bit more to taste the more expensive and acclaimed "reserve" wines ($25 and up is common), and the best of those experiences are sit-down private appointments with a winemaker that can last an hour or more. Generally, it's a good idea to budget an hour and a half for each visit, unless a wine-maker specifies otherwise. If you want to visit several wineries, no one will mind in the least if you ask to share a flight with your tasting companions, and in many cases the cost of your tasting fees will be waived if you buy a bit of wine to take home with you.

In some places, especially in the smaller back-road wineries, there will be no charge for tasting and no charge even for the wine-maker tours, and there is never any obligation to buy wine. But winemaking is an expensive business, and for many of these small proprietors this is a labor of love. Buying someone's wine after you've enjoyed it is the best compliment, and my own rule of thumb for wine tasting etiquette is that, if there is no charge for the tasting, the polite thing to do is buy at least two bottles. When there is a charge for the tasting, I buy only the wines I know I will enjoy. But because tasting fees are so often waived with a pur-chase, it never makes any sense to me not to buy a bottle or two at each winery. If you don't have room to take it home, many of the best local restaurants here in wine country charge only a modest corkage fee for opening your own special bottle tableside.

Napa County is justly famous for its restaurants, which include some of the finest dining experiences anywhere—and often at equally rarified prices. But it's also possible to eat sumptuously here in the wine country on a budget, and the streets of small towns like Yountville, St. Helena, and Calistoga are filled with excellent bistros, where the industry insiders gather after the tasting rooms close to enjoy a good meal and small-production wines.

In the summer, there are local farmers' markets up and down Highway 29, and the evening Chef's Market in downtown Napa (currently Thursdays), where you can shop for regional delicacies and listen to live music, has been part of the city's gourmet renaissance in recent years. The local grocery stores and specialty shops are stocked with an astonishing variety of artisanal meats, cheeses, and produce, where you can find all the fixings for an impromptu vineyard picnic.

The restaurant recommendations in this guide highlight places where you are welcome to enjoy your most recent discovery for a modest corkage fee. These are invariably also places that have excellent local wine lists, where perhaps new discoveries await. In many cases I suggest unique small-lot wines that are on the wine lists at my favorite places—wines made by people whose production is so limited that there are no tasting rooms at all. These are highly acclaimed wines that you wouldn't otherwise be able to sample, although you can order them directly from the winemakers if you're looking to add something special to your cellar. Above all, of course, in a part of the world where fine dining is a serious undertaking, these are restaurants where you can settle in for a relaxed and delicious long afternoon lunch or where you can celebrate that special occasion with a bottle of something that you'll never find back home.

Wine Tasting Essentials

EVEN SOPHISTICATED WINE AFICIONADOS sometimes find themselves wondering what the "right" way to taste wine is, and, as you anticipate sitting down face-to-face with a winemaker, it's easy to start worrying about whether you'll pass the test. There's no need: in the wine country, the friendliest welcome of all is reserved for passionate amateurs. You're not the only one who gets the giggles when that gentleman at the far end of the tasting bar starts throwing around wildly improbable adjectives either.

However, if you want to refresh yourself on the basics before embarking on your wine tasting adventures, it's easily done. For starters, hold the wine glass by the stem. Cupping it in your hands and leaving greasy fingerprints not only looks decidedly unglamorous but will also warm the wine, which changes its aromas. The experts will tell you that "tasting" wine is largely about aroma. We can experience only six different tastes, and nature's way around the limited range of our taste buds is to marry those perceptions to the thousand or more different smells that we can detect, creating seemingly endless delights for the gourmet. This is the whole point of swirling and sniffing your wine.

When you are handed a glass—and your tasting typically will progress from the lightest wine to the most intense wine in the flight—begin by gently tilting it to look at the clarity and color. Unless you're an expert, the conclusion you'll probably reach is that it looks delicious, but a trained eye will be looking to assess alcohol content, barrel aging, and structural components. Then, give the glass a swirl. Many of us accomplish this most gracefully by keeping the glass on the table and making a few quick circles, but if you're the daring sort, there's always the riskier midair execution to perfect as the afternoon wears on. The point is that the movement begins to open the bouquet of the wine. You are supposed to start with a gentle sniff with your nose above the glass, then move on to a deeper sniff with your nose right down there in the stemware. As a wine drinker and not a contest judge, you're looking for a sensory experience that will help you pick out the different aromas that shape how this wine is going to taste for you.

The next step—finally—is to take a sip of wine. Remember that the taste buds are in your mouth and not down your gullet. So roll the wine around in your mouth for a few moments, making sure it reaches the different parts of your tongue, where the distinct tastes and textures are experienced. Before you swallow, you can also try pulling a little air over your teeth and breathing in through your nose to aspirate the wine and intensify the experience of the aroma.

There is also a technique where you can attempt to slurp the wine silently and draw the vapors into your sinuses, usually effected by placing your tongue on the outside of the glass as you drink and inhaling simultaneously. If you do it right, the result is what the experts call retro-olfaction—a concentrated explosion of aroma that takes the information your brain needs to process smell more directly to your neurological receptors—but if you do it wrong, you'll end up sputtering wine rather dramatically. It might be wise to practice at home first, or, if you find yourself wine tasting without an audience, ask one of the winemakers to show you how it's done.

You may also see some fellow tasters spit the wine out without swallowing in the course of your tasting adventures. That's perfectly acceptable, and it's the reason all tasting rooms have those dump buckets on the counter. Those little sips of wine add up quickly, after all. If you're lucky enough to be invited to a barrel tasting, spitting is de rigueur. These are wines still in the making, and no one expects them to be of a finished, drinkable quality. Barrel tasting is an exceptional opportunity to learn about how the structure and aromas of a wine develop over time. Winemakers are happy to explain what is happening with a wine at any given moment, and learning to judge how a wine evolves is an essential element of connoisseurship. And remember: no matter how much fun you are having, drinking from the dump bucket happens only in the movies.

Shipping Wines Home

FOR MANY VISITORS TO NAPA, the trouble is finding ways to get all these wonderful wines home. And when you have been touring the back lane wineries, discovering small-production, handcrafted wines that won't be available at home, the question takes on a particular urgency. Most of the wineries in this book distribute their wines only through their tasting room sales, and this is part of what makes discovering them so satisfying.

Depending on where you live, there are several excellent options for getting your purchases back to your home cellar. Many wineries will ship your purchases home to you directly, provided your state allows this. The costs are generally prohibitive for a single bottle of wine, but for several it is quite reasonable. For purchases of a case or more, ask whether there is flexibility in their wine club program. The discounts are significant if you are a member, and generally your only commitment is agreeing to purchase a case of wine over the course of the year. Often, the wineries want to ship the wines to you quarterly, but, when I wanted to get a few cases to my summer place in New England, I never had any trouble persuading local winemakers to send me the entire annual allotment at once, at a significant savings in the shipping.

You can also ship the wines home directly through commercial freight companies, and there are a number of smaller shops that specialize in helping visitors to the wine country get their precious cargo safely to its destination. These shops often supply specially designed wine shippers for a minimal fee, and, if you live in a state where wineries are prohibited from mailing wines directly to consumers, this may be your best option for sending a case or two home ahead of you. The price for shipping a case, without insurance, to the East Coast generally runs around $80, with prices less for shorter distances. At the end of this book, I list some shops that I have found particularly easy to work with.

Another option is to send the wine as checked luggage, and this is frankly my favorite. I have done it for years and only rarely has a bottle broken en route. A sturdy cardboard box, marked fragile, can get an entire case of wine across the country with minimal hassle, provided you understand the airline policies and any unusual state sales-tax regulations (available from your local bureau of taxation). Most wineries will happily give you a regular packing box, and some of the wineries have started selling extra-sturdy boxes specifically designed for sending wines this way. Some wineries now sell cleverly designed wine "sleeves" of inflatable plastic perfect for slipping a bottle or two into a bag—or you can purchase a "wine-lover's suitcase" from catalog suppliers before your trip and rest easy knowing that your only worry is finding favorite bottles to fill it up.

For those extra-special, high-end purchases destined for the cellar of the serious collector, there are always third-party shippers who specialize in sending wines anywhere you need them to go. On page 230, I list my favorite ones, or you can ask at any premium winery for recommendations.

And here's my favorite wine country secret: You can fly on several commercial airlines directly in and out of the airport in Santa Rosa, over in neighboring Sonoma County. In addition to saving the hour-and-a-half drive from the Bay Area airports and starting your wine country weekend that much sooner, Horizon Air (an Alaska Airlines partner) doesn't currently charge you for the first case of wine shipped home as checked luggage (details at sonomacountyairport.org).

Even if you take nothing home with you as a souvenir for your cellar, the back lane wineries of Napa are an experience few visitors ever forget. Off the beaten path and along the back roads, amid oak trees and mustard blooms, the experience of wine tasting is immediate and personal. May your journey and discoveries be as individual as your palate, and welcome to the heart of the Napa Valley.

CHAPTER 1
DOWNTOWN NAPA AND ENVIRONS

WINERIES

PROVISIONS

Maps on pages xii–xiii

THE FIRST NATIVE AMERICAN INHABITANTS of this region were the Wappo, who named the valley the "land of plenty"—or Napa. Those who have since settled in this magical corner of the world have been struck by the same sense of its special bounty. The wine country to the north of San Francisco was renowned in the 1850s and 1860s for its gold and silver, which led to some of California's most fabled mining rushes and to the establishment of many of the small towns that tourists enjoy today.

During the latter years of the nineteenth century and throughout the twentieth century, the Napa Valley was famous for its fruit production—part of which already included, by the 1870s, the region's acclaimed vineyards. But it wasn't until the 1970s that Napa became America's most recognizable wine country.

While the county of Napa and the wines made here have international recognition, visitors are often less familiar with the city of Napa, which is the gateway to the tasting trail. In your travels, it's worth a stop. In recent years, the city has been undergoing an urban renaissance, and today it is a vibrant small community with some of the area's best local produce, small family restaurants, and engaging evening entertainment. During the warm summer evenings, families (and visitors) stroll the streets, taking in some of the live music or making impromptu meals in the al fresco markets. Best of all, of course, there are an increasing number of small tasting rooms right in the heart of the city, where you can continue making some discoveries after hours. This section also includes the back lane wineries clustered just to the east of Napa, in the newest AVA in the county—Coombsville.

A DECADE OR SO AGO, downtown Napa was a sleepy place on a Friday night. Today, it's one of the wine country's hottest spots on a balmy evening. And the folks at Ceja Vineyards were among the earliest pioneers in this urban renaissance. Their downtown tasting salon was one of the first to open a few years back. Now, you can easily spend an entire afternoon wandering through the tasting rooms, markets, and restaurants that have sprung up along the riverfront.

The Ceja (pronounced say-ha) family is also pioneer in another sense. They came to Napa from Mexico to work in the vineyards in 1967, and it was nearly twenty years before they purchased their own land in the Napa Valley. Today, the family—brothers Armando and Pedro, their wives Martha and Amelia, and several of their children—operate one of California's first modern wineries to be established by Mexican immigrants.

The four co-owners have more than a hundred years of winegrowing experience among them; all grew up working in the vineyards. Pedro and Amelia met there as teenagers. These days, Ceja Vineyards is a flourishing enterprise looking forward to a second generation. Daughter Dalia's blog, The Ole! Report (theolereport.com), and son Navek's talent for design and video production are all part of the family's goal of bringing wine to the people in fun and innovative ways.

The family makes nearly a dozen different wines, ranging from Carneros Chardonnay and Pinot Noir wines to a Napa Valley Syrah and Pinot Noir blend. There's also a botrytis white Sauterne-style dessert wine of Sauvignon Blanc and Semillon for those who enjoy something special after dinner. A range of cooler-climate wines is made from estate-grown grapes from the Sonoma Coast. The total annual production is around seventy-five hundred cases, and the wines range from $20 to $50 a bottle. The tasting fee is $10.

MARK HEROLD WINES

701 First Street, Napa
Exit Highway 221 north from
Highway 29, east on First
Street, at Oxbow Market

Tel. 707.256.3111,
markheroldwines.com

Tasting daily 1 p.m.
to 5:30 p.m.

WHEN YOU TALK TO PEOPLE in the know in Napa, the names of a couple of winemakers come up time and time again. They are spoken of with a mixture of admiration and reverence. These are folks who, somehow, seem to be able to turn grapes into something that isn't just wine but the kind of wine that is an experience. Mark Herold is one of those names, and he is the winemaker at some of the wine country's highest flying estates. Mark first made his name crafting small-lot cult wines in his garage back in the late 1990s, and just recently he's opened a tasting room to continue that tradition of making a few special wines under his own label.

The wines here are undeniably eclectic, and Mark sources his fruit from different handpicked locations around California, including vineyards in Lake and Mendocino counties (to the north of Napa and Sonoma, respectively) and Lodi (at the northern end of the Central Valley to the south). There are some Spanish-style reds, made with blends of Tempranillo, Petite Sirah, Carignane, and Graciano that harken back to the mission tradition that first made Northern California a wine country; some Rhône- and Spanish-style white and rosé wines (mainly Grenache led) for summer drinking; and of course, some of the very serious and luscious Cabernet Sauvignons that Mark is known for. The price range of the wines varies accordingly, from around $20 to $40 for the blends to approaching $200 for the Cabernet wines.

The tastings ($20) are flexible, depending on your interests and pocketbook, and you're welcome to browse the extensive and well-thumbed wine library. The entire experience has the urban hip aura that is starting to make downtown Napa a go-to spot in the valley. It's next door to the Oxbow Market (page 44), where you can also eat your way through a trove of local delights and pleasures.

THE FONTANELLA FAMILY WINERY is nestled in the western hills of Napa, on the southern tip of the Mount Veeder appellation, and owners Jeff and Karen Fontanella confess that they might have been just a bit delirious when they first decided to build a winery on the property. The process of negotiating the land-use permits alone took the couple two years. Fortunately, Karen came to the wine business after a career practicing real estate law. Jeff, meanwhile, had built a reputation working as a winemaker at some of the valley's big names, including Opus One and Saddleback. It seemed like the perfect opportunity to live part of the wine country dream.

Today, the Fontanella tasting room and winery, which opened to the public in the summer of 2008, is one of the county's charming pastoral retreats. The tasting room looks out over a tranquil pond, and there are views of the hills in the distance. On cooler days, guests settle in around the fireplace, and in the summer months tasting takes place al fresco on the long back patio. The couple runs the tasting room, and Jeff, of course, is the winemaker, so this is an intimate and personal experience, where visitors get a chance to meet the people behind the wines and perhaps make some new friends in the valley.

Currently, Jeff and Karen make just three wines—a Chardonnay, a Zinfandel, and a Cabernet Sauvignon ($30 to $55)—and these are all small-lot wines, handcrafted from local fruit sources and from their own Cabernet Sauvignon estate vineyards on their twenty-six-acre bit of paradise.

FROM THE HILLTOP ESTATE at Caldwell Vineyards, there are views of the Napa Valley in both directions. You can see as far as the Carneros if you look one way, and the peak of Mount St. Helena if you look the other. In the foreground, of course, there are vineyards—fifty-seven acres of them. When John Caldwell bought this property in the 1980s, his first idea was to subdivide and resell. Transforming this unique corner of the Napa Valley into an estate winery came later, after he had fallen in love with this bit of earth.

These days the family—John and his wife, Joy, along with his father, Jack, and wife, Alma—produces around thirty-five hundred cases a year on a ranch that John likes to joke doesn't have a naturally flat place on it. Caldwell Vineyards has built its reputation working with unusual clones, and the focus is on keeping the wines as purely expressive as possible. This means that winemaker Marbue Marke prefers traditional artisanal methods such as whole berry and barrel fermentation.

But there's a bit more to the Caldwell clonal story as well. Back in the 1970s, John smuggled some of these vines in from France in a story that's full of high drama and intrigue. You want to be sure to ask him the story

CALDWELL VINEYARDS

169 Kruezer Lane, Napa
Exit Highway 221 north
from Highway 29, east
on Highway 121

Tel. 707.255.1294,
caldwellvineyard.com

Tasting by appointment only

about how he ate—that's right, ate—the incriminating receipts some Canadian customs officers found in the trunk of his vehicle crossing the border. Or about how he hid the vines from the authorities by burying them under an old oak tree on the property. Eventually, realizing that the life of a smuggler was fraught with peril, John took up legal importing and became the first winemaker in the country to grow vines brought over from some of the world's most prestigious French vineyards.

Wine devotees will still appreciate the Caldwell clonal-variety collection. The vineyard produces wines in three collections. They make a small amount of a signature ultra–premium Napa Valley wine, including a Cabernet Sauvignon and a Cabernet and Syrah blend (ranging from $120 to $225). Their varietal clone collection ranges from great summer wines like Sauvignon Blanc or a rosé of Syrah to the Cabernet Sauvignon clones John made famous ($40 to $120). There is also an excellent proprietary red "Rocket Science" blend (around $50).

Private tasting appointments include a tour of the underground winery, a chance to take in the views, and time to sample the wines, which the family pairs with local cheeses and expert conversation. There are only a small number of tasting appointments per month, and the tasting fee ($45 and up generally) varies depending on your interest.

PORTER FAMILY VINEYARDS

1189 Green Valley Road, Napa
Head east on Coombsville
Road from Highway 121
until Green Valley Road
intersection

Tel. 707.265.7980,
porterfamilyvineyards.com

Tasting by appointment only

A COUPLE OF MILLION YEARS or so ago, Coombsville—that hillside cauldron dug out of the Napa Valley in the area between Mount George and Stag's Leap—was seashore property. Today, it rises five hundred feet above sea level and is increasingly renowned for its excellent production of Cabernet Sauvignon wines.

When Tom and Bev Porter left Silicon Valley to purchase their twenty-acre hillside vineyard property back in 2005, they set about excavating an underground cellar and production facility, and in the process discovered the fossilized footprints of ancient shorebirds. An image of those prehistoric sandpiper tracks appears on the labels of the Porter Family Vineyards wines, including their flagship Cabernet Sauvignon and robust Syrah (in the $50 to $95 range). The family also releases a limited production of rosé wine, a Chardonnay, and a couple of proprietary blends (from $20 to $40), for a total estate wine production of just over two thousand cases.

Now a two-generation family business, son Tim today runs the winery, and, as chance would have it, all the Porters have a scientific bent. This means that vineyard management on the property is high-tech. These steep hillside vineyards exhibit a variety of microclimates on the estate, which has been divided into thirty micro blocks, each with different soil depths and water needs taken care of by a state-of-the-art wireless irrigation system, a vineyard sensory mesh network, and weather stations. There are thoughts of giving each plant in the vineyard its own radio-controlled identification tag. This is where science meets winemaking at its most ingenious.

But technology doesn't get in the way of the down-to-earth business of growing grapes up here in the mountain valleys above Napa. A visit to the Porter Family Vineyards includes a family-hosted tour of the vineyards and the caves and a behind-the-scenes introduction to how a great wine is produced. There's also a chance to sample some wines, of course. The charge for the hour-and-a-half private tour is $40.

ANCIEN WINES

4047 East Third Street, Napa
Head east on Coombsville
Road from Highway 121, north
on Third Street until East Third
Street intersection

Tel. 707.255.3908,
ancienwines.com

Tasting by appointment only

OWNED AND OPERATED by Ken Bernards and his wife, Teresa, Ancien Wines specializes in making hand-crafted Pinot Noir, Pinot Gris, and Chardonnay wines ($27 to $58), which Ken discovered a passion for in the 1980s when he was completing a chemistry degree at Oregon State University, in the heart of the Willamette Valley wine country.

Ancien is located east of the city of Napa, where few tourists ever come, on the site of the historic Haynes vineyards. The property has had working vineyards on it since 1885, when the Haynes family purchased it from Nathan Coombs, one of the first white settlers in the Napa Valley. The original vineyards were destroyed in the fires that spread after the great San Francisco earthquake of 1906, but, in 1966, Duncan and Pat Haynes replanted the property to Pinot Noir and Chardonnay under the tutelage of Napa wine pioneer Louis Martini Sr., making it one of the oldest Pinot Noir and Chardonnay vineyards in California. Blocks of these early vines are still in production today.

The winemaker's tour includes a walk through the vineyards and, in the warmer months, a tasting under the oak trees, with views of Mount George and the foothills of the Vacas range. During the rainy months, you'll sample by candlelight in the barrel room at a small wooden table. In addition to the wine produced from fruit grown here in the Haynes vineyards, Ken also sources Pinot Noir from other spots in the Carneros AVA, Sonoma County, the Willamette Valley, and the Santa Rita Hills.

Best of all, if you're looking to learn more about the wines that you are discovering here in the Napa Valley, the tasting experience at Ancien is one of the best educational opportunities in the county. The winery welcomes everyone from serious Pinot Noir collectors to new enthusiasts looking for a crash course in Wine 101. There's a chance to do barrel tasting and to learn firsthand how different barrels made at different cooperages affect the flavor of the wines. You'll learn about head-pruned vines and what makes an Alsatian-style Pinot Gris and how the afternoon breezes shape the microclimate. The hour-and-a-half tour and tasting has a fee of $40 per person, waived for members—new or old—of their wine club.

GRASSI WINE COMPANY

1213 Coombs Street, Napa
Tasting off-site; call for details

Tel. 707.244.7142,
grassiwines.com

Tasting by appointment only

MARK AND JAMI GRASSI, with the help of their daughter, Cassandra, make just a handful of wines, but they first came to national attention with their small-lot premium Cabernet Sauvignon ($60), which earned a rating in the 90s from *Wine Spectator* in the first year it was released (2008). They also make an aromatic white wine from the Italian varietal Ribolla Gialla and a luscious Sangiovese-and-Merlot blend that they call Mezzo/Mezzo—or half-and-half. Success like this in an area of the world richly blessed with glorious wines—and especially in a region renowned as Cabernet country—makes these wines to watch. They have remained consistently stellar producers, and, if you're looking for something rare and wonderful to take home, something no one else will have heard about, here's your chance.

Part of the secret of the Grassi success is the family vineyards, of course. Devotees of Cabernet Sauvignon won't be surprised to learn that Silver Oak—something of a legend in Napa County—has a hundred acres of vineyards just behind their property. All the fruit is grown on-site here in the Atlas Peak AVA, and, with winemaker Robbie Meyer (the other part of the Grassi secret), the family makes a wine handcrafted from vineyard to bottle. There is no charge for tasting, and one percent of all proceeds are donated to environmental protection under the One Percent for the Planet program.

MARK POPE is a self-described cross between catalog pioneer J. Peterman, humorist Tom Bodett, and counterculture journalist Hunter S. Thompson, and he is a man with enough irons in the fire to keep all three of those gentlemen intrigued. In addition to his wine catalog sales and impressive range of private-label wines, Mark runs one of the quirkiest wine bars, BBQ joints, and wine retail shops in Napa.

Here, you'll find a judicious selection of wines made by the valley's best small vintners, as well as the small-lot wines that Mark buys from contacts in the industry and produces under his own labels, including his flagship Justice (the motto is "Justice Is Served"). If you couldn't fit in as many tasting appointments out on the back lanes as you were hoping, here's a chance to taste some more small-production wines from around the world over a casual lunch or dinner.

If you're hankering for some down-home dining, the menu offers premium meats, cooked out back on the Southern Pride Smoker, including beer-can chicken and Kobe beef burgers (under $20). On weekends, BBQ is served until midnight.

As you would expect from a place where luxury meets blue-jeans style, the ambience alone is worth the trip. The bar rail is an 1887 railroad track from Sheffield, England, and the ceiling is hand-stamped Mexican tin. At the end of one of the tables, an old riding saddle does double duty as a barstool. It's an eccentric, fun watering hole, where you can try out some local wines (or the hand-selected single-barrel bourbons and fine tequilas) and share in the Far West vision of a corporate renegade gone cowboy.

IN THE HEART OF downtown Napa is the Oxbow Public Market, a sprawling, bustling temple of artisanal foods and local treasures. Here you'll find more than a dozen local purveyors selling everything from specialty teas and fresh-roasted coffees to baked goods, cheese, spices, and local wines. There are also a number of small restaurants and food stands, selling everything from tacos to fresh oysters from nearby Marin County, making it a top choice for a casual strolling dinner. Most vendors stay open late on Saturdays and on Tuesday "locals" nights, when there is live music along the riverfront. Don't miss a tasting at Mark Herold Wines here at the market (page 28).

RUN BY THE husband-and-wife team of Michael and Christina Gyetvan, Pizzeria Azzurro is a favorite spot in the wine country for wood-fired pizzas served up in a casual and friendly setting. This is the kind of neighborhood restaurant where locals stop by to pick up take-out for the kids and where folks come to celebrate birthdays with friends. There's also a chic wine bar where you can order up a satisfying meal of antipasti and bruschetta, a range of fresh salads, and some sinful desserts. Most entrees are priced $15 to $20. If you want to enjoy a bottle of your most recent discovery, corkage is just $15.

PIZZERIA AZZURRO E ENOTECA

1260 Main Street, Napa
North on Highway 221, west on Pearl Street, north on Main Street

Tel. 707.255.5552, azzurropizzeria.com

Open Sunday to Wednesday 11:30 a.m. to 9:30 p.m., Thursday to Saturday 11:30 a.m. to 10 p.m.

WALK INTO ZUZU and it's hard not to feel right at home. And that's just what the proprietor Mick Salyer was going for when he opened this Spanish-style tapas and paella spot in downtown Napa. There's upbeat Latin music on the stereo, a Mexican tin ceiling, and plenty of friendly faces usually gathered around the pine bar, enjoying some of Zuzu's small bites and a glass of wine.

The wines are small-lot back lane selections from California, Spain, Italy, Portugal, New Zealand, and South America, and there is an especially wide array by the glass. The food is excellent, with tapas that range from local fish samplings and Sonoma lamb chops to crab pastries, all served up Latin style ($5 to $15). The paella changes daily (around $10 per person). Large groups can enjoy the family table upstairs with views over the Napa River.

ZUZU TAPAS AND PAELLA

829 Main Street, Napa
North on Highway 221,
west on Third Street,
north on Main Street

Tel. 707.224.8555,
zuzunapa.com

Lunch Monday to Friday
11:30 a.m. to 2:30 p.m.

Dinner Monday to Thursday
4:30 p.m. to 10 p.m.,
Friday 4 p.m. to 11 p.m.,
Saturday 4 p.m. to 11 p.m.,
Sunday 4 p.m. to 9:30 p.m.

CHAPTER 2
SILVERADO TRAIL
including Stag's Leap and Oak Knoll

WINERIES

Maps on pages x–xi and xii–xiii

THE SILVERADO TRAIL runs along the eastern side of the Napa Valley, roughly parallel to the more familiar St. Helena Highway, and connects the city of Napa to the south with Calistoga nearly thirty miles to the north. It was originally established in the nineteenth century as a wagon trail linking the mercury and silver mines on Mount St. Helena with San Pablo Bay and San Francisco, and today it is the one of the wine country's two main tourist itineraries.

More than thirty wineries are clustered along the Silverado Trail, and the road passes through acres of vineyards, making it a popular route for visitors whose tastes run toward the more bucolic. On summer weekends, especially, the traffic and the tasting rooms—although hardly vacant—are often much less congested here than in the more familiar corners of the valley. In the middle parts of the trail, there is only one real convenience store and dining option, the quaint and rustic Soda Canyon Store (4006 Silverado Trail, sodacanyonstore.com), and there are almost no gas stations to be found out here, so be sure to fill up the tank before starting out, especially if you plan to go wine tasting over in the mountain valleys, which can be a long way up in the hills. You may want to plan your tasting appointments with a good break for lunch back on the beaten path or pick up the fixings for a gourmet roadside picnic. Once you've got the details arranged, there's a whole day to enjoy the sunshine and scenery and some of that famous wine.

WHITE ROCK VINEYARDS

1115 Loma Vista Drive, Napa
Tasting off-site; call for details

Tel. 707.257.7922,
whiterockvineyards.com

Tasting by appointment only

THE NAME OF THIS WINERY comes from the white volcanic ash found in the soil on the property, and if you've ever been interested in having an insider's look at the volcanic elements of terroir, the White Rock caves are a lesson in and of themselves. The geological striations found along the walls and ceilings of the caves—which range from black lava and red magna to that signature white ash—tell the history of what makes Napa such a uniquely prosperous wine-growing region.

Early settlers started making wine on the site of White Rock Vineyards, here in a small valley at the foot of the Stag's Leap range, back in the 1870s. The Vandendriessche family has been carrying on that tradition in pastoral seclusion since the 1970s. The winery is located down the end of a small lane, well off the beaten path, and you won't find any sign pointing the way. Instead, the property is just a broad expanse of vineyards and oak trees, dotted with the occasional palm tree and distant barn.

When you arrive, there's nothing pretentious. There is a small laboratory out front, where a bit of the chemistry that it takes to make a great wine happens, and visitors gather around a small bar tucked back into the underground caves that serve as the production facility and storage rooms at White Rock. Today, building caves is something of a fashion in the wine country, but the Vandendriessche family built theirs twenty years ago. Organic and biodynamic farming is also on the rise in the Napa Valley, but these vineyards have been managed without herbicides since the 1970s. The result is a winery that feels very much a part of the scenery that surrounds it, and that's part of the spirit at White Rock Vineyards.

Owners Claire and Henri released their first commercial vintage back in the mid-1980s, and they first made their reputation as excellent producers of what they call their Napa Valley Claret. In *The Wine Advocate*, Robert Parker praised the 2001 vintage for its "distinctive Bordeaux-like personality" and awarded it 90 points. For the first eighteen years, they made just that one red wine and a small-lot production of Burgundian-style Chardonnay, with just a whisper of oak. Today, sons Christopher and Michael are now part of the second generation of family winemaking at White Rock, and the Vandendriessches have added two more Cabernet Sauvignons, including a reserve wine sold only from the tasting room ($80). There is the occasional release to wine club members of extremely small lots of other wines—sometimes as few as a half-dozen cases—including Viognier, Malbec, Syrah, and a reserve Chardonnay. Most wines are from $30 to $50, with a total production of around three thousand cases, and there is no charge for a visit.

ROBERT BIALE VINEYARDS

4038 Big Ranch Road, Napa
Exit Salvador Avenue east
from Highway 29, north on
Big Ranch Road

Tel. 707.257.7555,
robertbialevineyards.com

Tasting by appointment only

IN *THE WINE ADVOCATE*, Robert Parker has called this little winery one of the most elite Zinfandel producers in California, and, if you want to taste how wonderful a Zinfandel wine can be, this is the place to come. Robert Biale was one of the leaders in the Zinfandel revolution of the 1990s, and today the winery's emphasis is still on single-vineyard-designate wines that express the full range of complexity locked up in this versatile grape.

The Biale family has deep roots in the wine country, with the father-and-son team of Aldo and Robert together running the vineyards that Aldo's father, Pietro, started in 1937. Around the beginning of the twentieth century, Pietro came to Northern California from Italy, and, after moving to the valley to work a ranch up on Mount Veeder, the family settled on a farm in the town of Napa and planted their vineyards. When Pietro died in a quarry accident in the 1940s, it was left to his teenage son and his widow to run the farm, which the young man did with some verve.

In fact, coming down the lane to the vineyard you'll notice signs with its signature Black Chicken icon, the name of one of the Zinfandels. It's also a nod to Aldo's scofflaw entrepreneurial pluck: Aldo, in his youth, made some delicious homebrew wines from those vineyards—wines that he might have possibly sold without exactly the correct licenses and permits. Back then, telephones used party lines, and, if a caller mentioned how many black chickens were needed, the wine would find its way.

Today, it's Robert Biale and his schoolmate, business partner, and marketer Dave Pramuk at the helm of the Biale winery. It produces about ten thousand cases of wine per year from the ten-acre estate vineyards in the Oak Knoll District, from the property known simply as "Aldo's Vineyard," and from a variety of historic vineyards, including a block in Sonoma's legendary Monte Rosso vineyard, where some say world-class winemaking in California got its start in the late nineteenth century.

About 80 percent of the production is in the Zinfandel that has made the winery famous. *Food & Wine* magazine has, in recent years, twice rated the Black Chicken label as the best Zinfandel over $20 in California. There is also a small production of Syrah and Petite Sirah. Wines range from around $40 to $75, with special pricing (and exclusive event invitations) for the fanatical regulars known as the Black Chicken Society. The charge for a tasting in the working winery, where you can look out over the vineyards and mustard blooms, is $10.

JUDD'S HILL

2332 Silverado Trail, Napa
North of the Monticello Road
intersection

Tel. 707.255.2332,
juddshill.com

Tasting by appointment only

THERE ARE FEW PLACES in the Napa Valley where tasting is more convivial than at Judd's Hill. After a meandering drive up through the vineyards, you'll find yourself sitting around a long wooden table, sipping wines and sharing jokes with new compatriots, who often come from far-flung places around the world. At Judd's Hill, the emphasis is on making wines personally and on creating a personal connection with the people who drink it.

Two generations of the Finkelstein family are at the heart of this family estate: founders Art and Bunnie; their son, Judd; and daughter-in-law, Holly. Art got his start in winemaking in the early 1970s, making garage wine with his brother in Los Angeles. They took the wines on the county fair circuit, started bringing home the ribbons, and, before long, went into the wine business together, founding Whitehall Lane. By the late 1980s, the business had grown and was too large to satisfy Art's passion for making small-lot, handcrafted wines, so they sold the winery and started up again at Judd's Hill, with the intention of making just a few thousand cases a year of the wines they enjoyed the most—Sauvignon Blanc, a summer rosé, Pinot Noir, Petite Sirah, and, of course, a Napa Valley Cabernet Sauvignon (wines around $20 to $75).

The emphasis on the personal, however, goes beyond the tasting room. Judd's Hill hosts a series of lighthearted events throughout the year, and, while wine club members have priority, the remaining tickets are offered to the public. A lobster luau is held in August, a Hanukkah hootenanny in December, and wine cruises up and down the Napa River scheduled around harvest. Those interested in joining the fun can check the website for details. While you're on the website, don't miss taking a peek at the weekly installment of Judd's Enormous Wine Show—an insider's comic view on the world of wine.

If you want to take home wine with your own stamp on it, Judd's Hill also offers another hands-on opportunity to learn a bit more about the art of winemaking and to make your own custom-crafted wines: the Bottle Blending Day Camp. In most cases, the process starts with a blending seminar, with the winemaker guiding you through the process of mixing different varietals to balance the flavors and components of a finished wine, and ends with you bottling and corking your take-home vintage (prices from $225).

The tasting fee at Judd's Hill is $15, waived with a purchase of $45. Unlike many places in the valley, the winery is kid friendly.

CASA NUESTRA WINERY

3451 Silverado Trail,
St. Helena
North of the Deer Park Road
intersection

Tel. 707.963.5783,
casanuestra.com

Tasting by appointment only

CASA NUESTRA MEANS "our house," and a folksy country welcome is the hallmark at this small and progressively run winery owned by Gene Kirkham and Cody Gillette Kirkham—the good friends and former marital partners who first established Casa Nuestra back in 1979. Located down a gravel lane on the west side of the Silverado Trail, the tasting room is a quirky old farmhouse, where bellying up to the bar means gathering in front of weathered boards set out across a vintage desk.

The philosophy here is that wine is liquid art and that community values are what sustain us. The wooden packing boxes are constructed by a local company that employs the disabled, and the clothing with the winery logo is made from hemp and bamboo. The grapes in the vineyards out back are grown organically, and, in these days when water is becoming a scarce commodity in California, Casa Nuestra is moving toward dry farming—raising grapes without any supplemental irrigation.

Apart from local restaurant sales, distribution is almost exclusively from the tasting room, and, if you're looking for a chance to try some rare varietals and unusual blends, Casa Nuestra has a lot to offer. Thirty-five years ago, the winery developed one of the first Cabernet Franc programs in North America, and many of the other vines it grows—Alicante Bouché, Carignane, French Colombard—remain specialty grapes in Napa. The estate Chenin Blanc has been praised by *Wine Spectator*'s Matt Kramer as the "finest and truest California Chenin Blanc"; other favorites include a dry rosé, a Tinto Classico red blend, an old-vine Petite Sirah, a dry Riesling, and a special late-harvest French

Colombard (wines from around $20 to $60). For enthusiasts looking to sample these unconventional wines on a regular basis, good discounts are offered through the wine club, Club Casa.

The winemaker's tasting includes a walk down the lane to the estate winery, a tour of the vineyards, and a special vineyard surprise. Elvis Presley fans may remember that the opening scene of his 1962 film *Wild in the Country* was filmed in the wine country, and, that's right, this was the location. The tasting room includes an offbeat collection of Presley memorabilia, mostly donated by enthusiastic visitors to this small family winery. The total production is around two thousand cases a year.

HUNNICUTT WINES

3524 Silverado Trail North,
St. Helena
North of the Deer Park Road
intersection

Tel. 707.963.2911,
hunnicuttwines.com

Tasting Tuesday to Sunday
10 a.m. to 5 p.m.
by appointment only

JUSTIN HUNNICUTT STEPHENS released his first wines, a Cabernet Sauvignon and a Zinfandel, in 2004, but he was no stranger to the winemaking industry. His father started producing wines in the 1990s under the family's D. R. Stephens Estate label, which Justin also manages and co-owns. But Justin's first job in the business was learning the ropes in the cellars at one of the other local family wineries.

In 2004, Justin produced fewer than 250 cases of wine under the Hunnicutt label. Today, the focus is still on making small lots of premium wines, and the annual production currently is around 2,000 cases, focusing mainly on Cabernet Sauvignon, along with a Chardonnay, a Zinfandel, a Merlot, and a proprietary blend of Petite Sirah called Fearless Red (wines from around $40 to $125). For those looking for something even more individual, you can also blend a barrel of wine yourself at Hunnicutt with the help of their winemaking experts.

The new Hunnicutt winery and tasting room is located on the Silverado Trail just a few minutes from downtown St. Helena. There, you can talk wines with Justin and his wife, Seana, (and eventually their children Parker, Preston, and Beckett) and enjoy discovering some new favorites in a relaxed environment. At Hunnicutt, you won't have to belly up to the bar and jostle your way to the wines: tasting takes place instead in an inviting seating area, and there are café tables overlooking the gardens and pine trees if you're looking to set a more leisurely pace. The regular tasting is $25, but there's also a tour-and-tasting package that includes a behind-the-scenes winery visit ($35). If you're feeling peckish, you can add some local charcuteries to the tour–and–tasting package ($50) and learn a bit about food-and-wine pairing. The fees for the tasting and tour are waived with the purchase of three bottles; the charcuterie package is free if you are a wine club member.

FAILLA WINES

3530 Silverado Trail,
St. Helena
North of Deer Park Road
intersection

Tel. 707.963.0530,
faillawines.com

Tasting by appointment only

RUN BY THE husband-and-wife team of Ehren Jordan and Anne-Marie Failla, Failla Wines (pronounced FAY-la) consistently produces world-class wines, but there's no mistaking that this is a family business. The *San Francisco Chronicle* named Ehren the 2008 winemaker of the year. *Wine Enthusiast* declared the Failla 2006 Napa Valley Phoenix Ranch Syrah the number one wine of the year on its Top 100 Wines list in 2008. But on weekends you are as likely as not to see their children riding bicycles out back.

The first estate vineyards for Failla were over on the Sonoma Coast, and in 2004 they purchased the ten-acre property just off the Silverado Trail. By 2008, Ehren and Anne-Marie had completed construction of an underground production facility and converted the old farmhouse into an inviting and cheerful tasting room. A visit to Failla still feels like being invited into a winemaker's home, and tasting often takes place sitting around a coffee table in comfortable armchairs and couches. In the summer, there is a shady veranda with views of the vineyards.

Ehren makes around five thousand cases of wine a year, mostly Sonoma Coast and Napa Valley Pinot Noir. There is also a smaller production of Chardonnay, Syrah, and Viognier. Wines range from around $35 to $65, and the $10 tasting fee is waived with purchase.

FOUNDED BY the husband-and-wife
team of Ernie and Irit Weir in 1979,
the wine country has grown up around
Hagafen Cellars. Today, this small family winery is surrounded by some of the
valley's great commercial giants, but the
Weirs have determinedly retained their
hands-on approach to the small-lot production of sustainably produced Napa

HAGAFEN CELLARS

4160 Silverado Trail, Napa
Just south of the Oak Knoll
Avenue intersection

Tel. 888.424.2336 ext. 113,
hagafen.com

Tasting by appointment only

Valley wines. The family grows walnuts and fruits in the orchard
out behind the tasting room (available free for the taking in season to tasting room visitors), and they keep an organic kitchen
garden on the property alongside the hen house, which produces an abundant supply of fresh organic farm eggs. The name
Hagafen comes from the Hebrew *borei pri hagafen*, which translates to "creates the fruit of the vine" and is the idea at the heart
of the Weirs' approach to the winemaking business.

Total production is eight thousand cases annually, and, in
addition to the more celebrated Napa Valley varietals, there's a
chance to taste wines made from some more eclectic fruit. You'll
find an estate-bottled Cabernet Sauvignon, a Cabernet Franc,
Syrah, and Riesling alongside a Roussanne and Tempranillo
(prices $15 to $75).

This is the kind of tasting room where everyone is welcome—
from serious collectors to first-time wine tasters. The feeling here
is low-key, casual, and friendly. The tasting fee is $10 for the cur-
rent release and $20 for the reserve tasting, both refunded with
your wine purchase.

HOURGLASS WINE

1104 Adams Street, Suite
103–104, St. Helena
Tasting off-site

Tel. 707.968.9332,
hourglasswines.com

Tasting by appointment only

UP A RURAL LANE off the Silverado Trail, past the vineyards, you'll come to the modernist tasting room that is home to Hourglass. Designed by the renowned San Francisco architect Ollie Lundberg, the building is built into the hillside, and what at many places is relegated to the sidelines—the wine production—here is deliberately front and center. After all, making a great wine is the first and last objective. There is an outdoor production room and crush pad where you'll often find winemaker Tony Biagi tasting, blending, and racking. It's a great chance to learn a bit about the technical side of winemaking and to ask all those lingering questions.

Proprietor Jeff Smith grew up here in Napa County, and part of this estate is land that his father, Ned, purchased back in the 1970s. Since then, he and his wife, Carolyn, have added to the acreage with some friends as partners and have built the new production facility and the caves that serve as their functional and beautifully atmospheric tasting room. One of the best things about working caves like this is that visitors get a chance to taste wines from the barrel, and barrel tasting is an education in itself. Jeff or one of his crew will be happy to walk you through the process if it's a new experience.

The emphasis at Hourglass is on the art of winemaking and education, so there are sample soil collections that give you a firsthand look at terroir and a chance to take a look underground at the different striations and geological formations that make this soil so perfect for premium wine production. Once you've had a chance to ask all your questions, there's also some of that signature Napa luxury on offer: the cave tasting room can only be described as subterranean swank.

Above all, the wines at Hourglass are stellar. The focus is on just over thirty-five hundred cases a year of premium Cabernet Sauvignon (most in the $100 to $160 range), along with traditional Bordeaux blending varietals.

PHIFER PAVITT WINE

4660 Silverado Trail, Calistoga
West of the Dunaweal Lane
intersection

Tel. 707.942.4787,
phiferpavittwine.com

Tasting by appointment only

SUZANNE PHIFER PAVITT and Shane Pavitt make just five hundred cases of two Napa Valley wines. Both the Sauvignon Blanc and the Cabernet Sauvignon are called DATE NIGHT and have become cult favorites. The Cabernet debuted with the 2008 vintage and comes from an organically farmed vineyard in Pope Valley. That wine earned stellar accolades: the *San Francisco Chronicle* ranked it in the year's top 100 wines, and *Wine Spectator* gave it an impressive 90 points. The debut release of the Sauvignon Blanc was 2011; it is sourced from a sustainably farmed Pope Valley vineyard as well.

While these are serious wine lovers' wines, the attitude at Phifer Pavitt is completely down-to-earth and light-hearted, a spirit reflected in everything from the cowgirl on the wine label to the relaxed atmosphere in the new tasting room, which embodies "eco-chic," with its blue-jean-stuffed walls, barbed-wire chandeliers, and recycled Wyoming snow planking on the walls. The wine gets its name from the couple's weekly date night, where they swear all the best decisions are made.

KIRK VENGE GREW UP in a winemaking family and got his introduction to managing vineyards riding around on tractors as a boy. From there, a life in the wine industry was a natural choice, and, after working a harvest Down Under and completing two degrees at the University of California Davis, he returned to the valley where he grew up.

VENGE VINEYARDS

4708 Silverado Trail, Calistoga
West of the Dunaweal Lane
intersection

Tel. 707.942.9100,
vengevineyards.com

Tasting by appointment only

Today, Kirk is the proprietor and winemaker at Venge Vineyards, just off the Silverado Trail, where he farms the twelve-and-a-half-acre property that he purchased in 2008. On the approach to the estate, visitors meander past neatly trimmed vineyards on the way up to the ranch house turned tasting salon, where dogs Lucy and Remy offer a friendly greeting and you'll get a chance to taste some wines. Kirk is passionate about making wines, and, if he's not out in the vineyards, it's easy to get him talking about what a bit of Charbono, Syrah, and Sangiovese add to his Zinfandel blend or how native yeasts help create wine with a unique sense of place.

At Venge, the production is fewer than four thousand cases a year. Kirk makes ten different wines, including a signature reserve Napa Valley Cabernet Sauvignon, a Chardonnay, and a late-harvest Zinfandel in the $25 to $125 range. From the sweeping shaded veranda of the tasting room, there are views across the valley to Diamond Mountain, and on a sunny afternoon it's a great spot to unwind a bit before returning to the back lane tasting trail.

JAMES COLE WINERY

5014 Silverado Trail, Napa
At Oak Knoll Ave

Tel. 707.251.9905,
jamescolewinery.com

Tasting daily 10 a.m. to 5 p.m.
by appointment only

IN THE BARREL ROOM at the James Cole Winery, what you see lined up along the walls is the entire vintage, and these are not wines you are going to find anywhere else. Because James Cole—the dream of James and Colleen Harder—still makes fewer than fifteen hundred cases a year, all of it sold directly from the winery. This is a strictly word-of-mouth sort of place, where you won't find balloons out front or gimmicks in the tasting room. The people who discover the Harders come back, vintage after vintage, and that's exactly the idea. The sign above the bar in the tasting room reads "enter as strangers, leave as friends."

James and Colleen met on a blind date after college, when James was on a business trip to Napa and Colleen was living in San Francisco. James had experience running a winery in his native Canada, and a mutual friend suggested, fatefully it would seem, that they meet for a glass of wine. When they later bought their estate vineyards and tasting room site here on the Silverado Trail, the property was a run-down horse ranch, which the couple has since transformed into a winery and chic tasting room. They currently make wines in the $40 to $150 range, including a 100 percent estate Cabernet Sauvignon, some small lots of 100 percent Malbec and 100 percent Petit Verdot, and a serious—and seriously drinkable—Chardonnay. The tasting experience (starting at $20) is hands-on and personalized, and, although the Silverado Trail is not precisely a remote back lane, James Cole is a far cry from the great din of the busy commercial wineries along this famous wine route.

SHAFER VINEYARDS

6154 Silverado Trail, Napa
Just south of Yountville
Cross Road

Tel. 707.944.2877,
shafervineyards.com

Tasting by appointment only

WHEN FOLKS START TALKING about the winemakers who changed the history of Napa in the 1970s and who put the wines from this narrow valley on the world map, the first names to come to mind might be Robert Mondavi, Louis Martini, or Bob Trinchero (who famously invented white Zinfandel). But, for many people in the valley, one of the names that comes to mind next is John Shafer. After serving with the Air Force and flying missions to Germany during the last months of the Second World War, followed by a career in publishing, he bought a 210-acre ranch in the wine country and moved his family west in 1972.

He was forty-eight years old, and, for the first six years the family grew grapes, while John threw himself into learning the craft of winemaking. His first commercial release of Cabernet Sauvignon won the prestigious San Francisco Vintners Club tasting competition. Within a decade, Shafer wines were outranking some of the legendary premier cru Bordeaux wines, at a moment when suddenly the wine world's attention was turning to Napa.

Currently, Shafer produces around thirty thousand cases of wine a year, and, with a stunning hillside tasting room right off the famed Silverado Trail, it would be hard to claim Shafer as an undiscovered secret. Today, run by John and his middle son, Doug, who worked as winemaker in the 1980s, this is very much still an intimate family business and an important part of the evolving Napa story. In the tasting room, wines are served in flights, with an array of gleaming glassware and gorgeous views over the vineyards. No jostling at a crowded tasting bar: this is a chance to participate in an expert wine seminar and see what a small family business can accomplish after forty years of hard work.

The family is still renowned for its Hillside Select Cabernet, an opulent wine made of 100 percent Cabernet that retails for more than $200. You'll also taste from their range of Chardonnay, Merlot, Cabernet, and Syrah wines, and they often pour samples of their recent production of 100 percent Hillside Cabernet port (most wines $50 to $70). Business travelers and home gourmets will appreciate the half-bottles, which make it possible to enjoy a fine wine for one or to enjoy a different vintage with every course. These are classic California wines with big, ripe flavors.

The winery is completely solar-powered, and the vineyard tour that begins the tasting takes place overlooking Stag's Leap. The fee for tasting is $55, and generally appointments need to be made several weeks in advance.

FROM THE TASTING BAR at Robert Sinskey, the view looks directly onto the working winery, and this integrated approach to the experience of wine is the hallmark of this family vineyard, which released its first vintage in 1986. Although the annual production is approaching twenty-five thousand cases, this is still a small, hands-on winery, the kind of place where come January everyone in the cellar takes a turn out back with the bottling.

Founded by Robert Sinskey *père* and now run by the husband-and-wife team of Robert Jr. and chef and cookbook author Maria Helm Sinskey, the vineyard produces wines from properties that are certified organic and farmed biodynamically, and the emphasis is—perhaps unsurprisingly—on making clean, easy-to-drink wines that pair well with great food. The tasting experience ($25) is accompanied by house-made hors d'oeuvres using Maria's recipes, and many of the ingredients come from the large gardens out in front of the winery. In autumn, the kitchens out back are busy canning and making some of the homemade fruit jams for sale in the winery. There are also a couple of premium food-and-wine tasting experiences (around $75), a wine-education tour (about $50), seasonal culinary tours, and occasional wine country cooking events. The tasting room was recently tapped by *Sunset* magazine as their Napa tasting room of the year, and for good reason.

From the vineyards, nearly two dozen wines are on offer, and these are small-lot productions—sometimes as little as forty or fifty cases. Robert Sinskey is known for their Pinot Noir wines made from properties over in the Carneros, but they also make several different Bordeaux blends, a range of white wines, a Vin Gris of Pinot Noir, and an especially delicious late-harvest Alsatian-style dessert wine made from Pinot Gris. As they will tell you in the winery, they are proud of the fact that there is no advertising budget at Robert Sinskey; their reputation for excellent wines has been built by word of mouth and by the friendly welcome visitors will discover.

PIÑA NAPA VALLEY

8060 Silverado Trail
North of Oakville Road

Tel. 707.738.9328,
pinanapavalley.com

Tasting daily 10 a.m. to 4 p.m.
by appointment only

THE PIÑA FAMILY has been farming vineyards in the Napa Valley for six generations, since the 1850s, and today four Piña siblings—John, Larry, Randy, and Davie—run this family winery. For many years, they made their fortunes in vineyard management, farming, and ranching. Then, in the 1960s, father John established a family estate here on the Silverado Trail. The brothers now source their grapes from select vineyards throughout the county.

The emphasis is primarily on single-vineyard-designate Cabernet Sauvignon blends (prices around $45 to $85), and recent releases have earned solid points in the 90s in places like *Wine Enthusiast*. They also make a lovely barrel-fermented Chardonnay (around $35). Wine tasting at the Piña winery includes a tour of the barrel rooms, where you can soak in the pungent, clean scent of oak and learn how a wine evolves in the aging and blending process. On summer days, there are patio tables and umbrellas where you can relax and look out over the Silverado Trail, and if you're lucky the fire pit will be burning, cooking up something special at one of the winery's club events or open houses.

CHAPTER 3
CALISTOGA AND ENVIRONS

WINERIES

PROVISIONS

DIVERSIONS

Maps on pages viii–ix

LOCATED AT THE FAR NORTHERN END of the Napa Valley, Calistoga is famous for its bottled water and its historic mineral hot springs, where you can soak away your cares and, some say, revitalize your health in waters heated by underground geysers. As the legend goes, the city got its name when the entrepreneurial pioneer Sam Brannan set about establishing a resort that he proposed to market to the world as the Saratoga Springs of California. By a slip of the tongue, Calistoga was born.

Today, Calistoga is also a laid-back and slightly offbeat place, with a charming main street, plenty of small restaurants, and some quirky boutique shopping. There are only a handful of tasting rooms set up in the town center, but there are plenty of small wineries tucked away on the outskirts of town, along the northern reaches of the St. Helena Highway and the Silverado Trail. If you're looking for a relaxed pace—made even more relaxing by a luxury spa treatment—it's a perfect place to while away an afternoon.

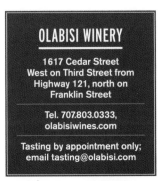

OLABISI WINERY

1617 Cedar Street
West on Third Street from
Highway 121, north on
Franklin Street

Tel. 707.803.0333,
olabisiwines.com

Tasting by appointment only;
email tasting@olabisi.com

THE SMALL WINERY run by Ted Osborne and Kim Wedlake is certainly worth a stop. Just be sure to contact them in advance in order to get first dibs on one of their coveted private tastings. Ted is a well-known winemaker here in the Napa Valley, having worked most recently for Storybook Mountain Winery, Piña Napa Valley (page 80), and Phifer Pavitt (page 70). In his years in the industry, he's also worked around the world, crafting vintages in Australia, France, and, of course, here in California. For his Olabisi label, established in 2002, Ted makes French-style Chardonnay, Syrah, and Petite Sirah wines, as well as, recently, some of the most exquisite Cabernet Sauvignon around. The industry experts are already in on the secret. James Laube of *Wine Spectator* describes the Olabisi wines as "ripe, rich wines that are remarkably elegant and graceful . . . Ted Osborne," he sagely observes, "shows a deft hand for crafting wines of subtlety and finesse. . . . This is a winery worth checking out."

Ted's emphasis is on exploring complexity in single-vineyard sites, working with a natural style, and crafting the ultimate expression of each vintage, in wines that range from $30 to $125 a bottle. The $25 tasting fee is credited toward your purchase. The name Olabisi, for those who are wondering, comes from an African girl's name meaning "joy multiplied."

THE MADRIGALS have been developing vineyard expertise here in Napa since the 1930s, when the first members of the family emigrated from Mexico to work the harvests. After decades of working in vineyard management and selling the fruit from their forty-acre estate property, the family—who realized that winemakers were earning accolades with the grapes they were growing—has now moved into winemaking as well. Madrigal released its first commercial vintage in 1995, a mere five hundred cases, and today their Petite Sirah wine (around $35) has a cult following in the valley.

Under direction of owners Jess and Chris Madrigal, the winery produces around five thousand cases of wine, which includes—in addition to their Petite Sirah—a range of Zinfandel, Merlot, Chardonnay, and Cabernet wines. *Wine Spectator* gave the reserve Cabernet—Las Viñas del Señor—a stellar 91 points in 2009, which has only added to this little winery's growing reputation.

The family has a tasting room just off the St. Helena Highway, where visitors are treated to a tour and tasting in the traditional California-style stucco winery. The estate vineyards begin out back, and the production takes place on site. The fee for tasting is $20.

SHYPOKE

2882A Foothill Boulevard
St. Helena Highway south of
Tubbs Lane intersection

Tel. 707.942.0420,
shypoke.com

Tasting by appointment only

CHARBONO is an Italian grape that genetic testing traces back to the Savoy region of France, where it was known as charbonneau. In California, it is often known as "Calistoga's Grape" because this northern corner of the Napa Valley is one of the world's best regions for growing this increasingly rare vine.

At Shypoke, the Heitz family, who has owned vineyard property in the Napa Valley since 1896, has been growing Charbono for more than a hundred years and is one of the wine country's largest producers of the varietal. They make around seven hundred cases a year. If you've never tried a Charbono—and chances are you haven't—a visit to this small, family-run winery is a chance to try something unique and wonderful.

A great-grandfather purchased this fifty-acre ranch at the end of the nineteenth century, and the family made wine from the Charbono vineyards until Prohibition put them out of business. While most of the property was converted to orchards, a couple of acres of the original vineyards survived, and in the 1950s they started replanting the land to grapes again, primarily Charbono with smaller lots of Cabernet Sauvignon, Grenache, Malbec, Sangiovese, and Petite Sirah.

Today, the winery is run by two generations of the Heitz family, who, because they don't have to pay a monstrous mortgage on a piece of vineyard property, can afford to produce excellent wines at very reasonable prices. The wines are all under $35.

The grapes are farmed using sustainable practices—the family says it doesn't want vineyards where they have to worry about their kids playing out back in the fields. The crush takes place in winemaker Peter Heitz's small barn in Calistoga using a hand-cranked basket press. The cool nights here in Calistoga produce fruits that ripen slowly. These are wines made with a light touch. The family also donates one percent of its sales to environmental causes.

There are vegetable gardens behind the house and free-range chickens in the vineyards, and, if you come when things are busy, you just might be put to work. If you're lucky, the wood-fired pizza oven will be going. The current production is right around a thousand cases, and there's no charge for a tasting appointment. The Shypoke name, they will tell you, comes from a local folk term for the blue herons that make their home along the river.

ZAHTILA VINEYARDS/ LAURA MICHAELS WINES

2250 Lake County Highway
North on Lake County
Highway from Highway 121

Tel. 707.942.9251,
zahtilavineyards.com

Tasting by appointment only

FOR CENTURIES, winemaking has largely been a man's world, and, until recently, that was true in the "new" wine country of Northern California as in the Old-World regions of France and Italy. Laura Zahtila Swanton is one of those rare early exceptions—but then she's never been one to follow the beaten path. After spending seventeen years working in the high-tech industry, she stumbled across a winery for sale, and it changed her life.

For a number of years, Laura ran the vineyard alone, determined to make a life in the wine world as a single woman. Not having grown up in the vineyards, she brought in consultant winemakers to help define the Zahtila house style. Then, in 2006, the man to whom she had been married in the early 1980s happened upon her winery website. In the way of fate and magical stories, it turned out they fell in love all over again decades later. They married for the second time in 2010, and today Laura and Michael Swanton are the very happy proprietors of Zahtila Vineyards and of the new Laura Michaels Wines, which is where they see their future heading.

Today, the couple makes about two thousand cases of premium Napa Valley wine—a Chardonnay, a rosé, their signature Zinfandels, some Cabernet Sauvignon, and a port. Wines start at under $20 and go up to $95 for the reserve Cabernet.

Tasting takes place at a redwood bar in a charmingly converted garage. Designed to resemble the traditional bar-style wineries that are so familiar on the back lanes of the wine country, the door to the tasting room is framed by an old wisteria vine. Out front, you'll find a profusion of hydrangeas and a sprawling rose garden, where Laura grows more than three hundred different rose plants that bloom in fragrant splendor from April through September. A gregarious Labrador meets you at your car to walk you to the tasting room, and there are plenty of winery cats luxuriating in the sunshine. The tasting fee ranges from $10 to $25, depending on how many wines you want to try. Because it's a small family operation, they look forward to welcoming you, but it's by appointment only.

ENVY WINES

1170 Tubbs Lane
North on Tubbs Lane
from Highway 128

Tel. 707.942.4670,
envywines.com

Tasting daily 10 a.m.
to 4:30 p.m.

A COLLABORATION between the talented winemaker Nils Venge and vintner Mark Carter, Envy Wines is one of a handful of back lane wineries tucked up on Tubbs Lane. Far from the hustle and bustle even of outposts like St. Helena and Calistoga, this is the perfect place to settle down with a picnic and a bottle of wine, which you can pick up here at the winery. Settle in long enough, and you can enjoy some additional natural excitement: there are views from the tasting room of Calistoga's Old Faithful Geyser (www.oldfaithfulgeyser.com), which erupts every half hour. The scent of lavender fills the air, and it's easy to imagine you are somewhere far off in Tuscany.

The best reason to come to Envy Wines isn't the views, fabulous as they are. These are serious, small-lot wines made by two masters and at prices that are hard to beat in the Napa Valley. Nils is a winemaker with a great reputation (his son, Kirk, inherited the family winemaking gene and is the proprietor at Venge Vineyards just down the Silverado Trail (page 71), and these are beautiful releases. Not too long ago, Nils garnered his second astonishing 100-point score (and Mark Carter his first) from *Wine Advocate*'s Robert Parker for one of the wines they crafted (the 2002 Carter Cellars To Kalon Cabernet Sauvignon). There are also Sauvignon Blanc and Petite Sirah wines, several Cabernet Sauvignon varietals and blends, a summer rosé, a port, and a late-harvest dessert wine. The prices range from $20 to $50, and Envy is also home to a few different labels, including Nil's private label, Vine Haven, and Mark Carter's highly regarded Carter Cellars. The tasting fee of $10 to $20 is waived with your purchase.

DALE AND MARLA BLEECHER both
lived in Italy before they moved to the
wine country, and their love story began
in an Italian class up north in Oregon.
So when they decided to establish their
own winery in the Napa Valley, it's no
surprise that the land they chose looks
like nothing so much as the hillside vineyards of Tuscany.

Except Dale and Marla will tell you
they didn't so much choose the land as the land chose them. At
Jericho Canyon they see themselves as the stewards of the grapes
and of the earth that nourishes them. That means everything is
done by hand in the vineyards, and the emphasis is on terroir and
varietal expression. And the terroir is dramatic and something special: these vineyards rise to nearly one thousand feet in elevation
with grades as steep as 45 percent, nestled in a magical little spot
between the Palisades range and Mount St. Helena.

The Bleechers raised their kids here, and their son, Nicholas,
has now joined them in the business after graduating from the
prestigious enology program at the University of California Davis.
Today, the family produces around fifteen hundred cases a
year, focusing on a few different hillside estate Cabernet Sauvignon wines (from $55 to $140), crafted in consultation with the
renowned winemakers Aaron Pott and Michel Rolland. They also
produce an estate olive oil made from the trees that surround
their home ($45). Visits are to their hillside tasting room, which
has spectacular views, and the experience is warm, friendly, and
hands-on.

UP VALLEY VINTNERS

1371 Lincoln Avenue
North on Lincoln Street from
Highway 29

Tel. 707.942.1004,
upvalleyvintners.com

Tasting daily noon to 5 p.m.

IF YOU'RE LOOKING for a chance to taste the wines of a number of small family vintners all in one place, Up Valley Vintners is the classic Napa co-op tasting room. Here, a group of back lane wineries share a single space, and there are regular monthly "meet-the-winemaker" afternoons (4 p.m. to 6 p.m.) if you want to make the personal connection.

The tasting room is relatively new, and at the moment there are four terrific wineries in the collective. Someday they might go as high as a half-dozen. You can't go wrong with these tastings. The tasting room is light and airy and comfortable, and the staff behind the bar could not be more friendly or welcoming.

You'll get a chance to try the Zacherle Wines, crafted by the husband-and-wife team of Nile and Whitney Zacherle. Nile Zacherle's first love wasn't wine but beer. Sometime well before he reached the age of twenty-one, he started making beer at home with his father, and, when he went off to college at the University of California, Davis, it was to study in the master brewers program. Along the way, he added a degree in fermentation science to his credentials as a master brewer. In the years since, Nile has worked as a winemaker at some of Napa's premium estates, including Barnett Vineyards (page 150), S. E. Chase (page 168), and the celebrated Château Montelena—whose

1973 vintage famously beat out its storied French competitors in the "Judgment of Paris." After taking some time to make wines in Bordeaux, France, and Margaret River, Australia, he teamed up with his wife, Whitney Fisher, also the winemaker and vineyards manager at her family's winery, Fisher Vineyards (page 154). Today, they are a high-powered winemaking couple, and both have earned stellar accolades, so it was only natural they would start their own label. They produce small lots of a couple of different wines, including a dry Riesling and a Pinot Noir from the Carneros and a Syrah from the Chalk Hill AVA. The wines range from $25 to $40.

This is also the tasting room for Tofanelli Vineyards, and many in the wine country were delighted when the third-generation grape grower Vince Tofanelli started producing a few hundred cases of his own wines too. Be sure to try the estate Charbono—made with a rare Calistoga varietal ($40; most wines $30 to $50). This is also the place for other hearty Italian reds, including a Zinfandel and Petite Sirah.

Kenefick Ranch Winery is the retirement dream of Dr. Thomas Kenefick, who, after a prestigious career as a neurosurgeon, now produces Bordeaux-varietal wines ranging from Cabernet Franc and Merlot to a Cabernet Sauvignon (prices from around $25 to $65). And Bar Smith, the proprietor at Barlow Vineyards, makes some super reds, as well as a rosé of Merlot and a Sauvignon Blanc that are worth notice (prices $20 to $50).

The modest tasting fee is $15, and there are often super specials on wines in the tasting room.

AUGUST BRIGGS WINERY

1307 Lincoln Avenue
North on Lincoln Avenue from
Highway 29

Tel. 707.942.5854,
augustbriggswines.com

Tasting daily 11 a.m.
to 5 p.m.; Tuesdays by
appointment only

ALONG THE QUAINT main street in downtown Calistoga—undoubtedly relaxed after a leisurely lunch or a long soak in one of the town's famous mineral hot springs—you'll see the tasting room of August Briggs, and it would be a shame to miss trying some of their wines.

This little winery was founded by August "Joe" Briggs, who produced his first commercial vintage back in 1995, after having worked for more than a decade in winemaking up and down the West Coast, where he developed a reputation for his skill with Pinot Noir. Just recently, however, Joe and his wife, Sally, retired and passed the reins of the family business over to nephew Jesse Inman and to three of the winery's longtime employees, who are now partners.

August Briggs currently produces around seven thousand cases of wine a year, sourced from twenty different vineyards. The Petite Sirah is grown in the two-acre estate vineyards just south of town, and there are a couple of different Pinot Noir wines, a few Cabernet Sauvignons, Chardonnay, Syrah, and—more unusually—both a Pinot Meunier and a local Charbono (most wines around $30 to $40).

Wine aficionados will recognize Pinot Meunier as one of the three grapes allowed in French Champagne production (the others being the more familiar Pinot Noir and Chardonnay varietals), and, although it is one of the most broadly planted grapes in France, you won't often find it bottled separately. Charbono, meanwhile, is known as "Calistoga's Grape," and, in the nineteenth and early twentieth centuries, it was a common varietal. Today, vineyards planted to the grape are dwindling, but the area's unique microclimate has long been recognized as an ideal area for growing this dark red grape, which boasts a distinctive plum aroma.

The August Briggs tasting room is a bright and airy space, and you'll find a warm welcome and an introduction to some of the finer points of winemaking. It's a great place to drop in and ask some questions. The folks pouring your wines are disarmingly good-natured and expert all at once—and likely as not they are one of the four partners, responsible for making the wine you get to enjoy.

THE RESORT at Solage Calistoga is delightfully posh, and if you are looking for a high-end, luxury retreat in the wine country, this is the place to go. But if your budget doesn't quite stretch to a couple hundred bucks for a spa treatment, do what the locals do and visit Solbar, the resort's Michelin-starred open-to-the-public restaurant for lunch, dinner, or a late afternoon cocktail. Most entrées at lunch are around $20, mains run $30 to $40 at dinner, and there's a good local wine list and some fun Napa-inflected cocktails. For something special, see if you can get a spot in one of their "Meet the Maker" winemaker dinners (around $130, food, wine, tax, and tip included) that are a local favorite in the valley (check the website for details and be sure to reserve in advance, as they book up quickly). You're just as likely to meet local vintners as you are tourists to the valley. Whether you pop in for an easy lunch or go all-out with the dinners, the setting is simply lovely. Best of all, if you need an afternoon diversion, there are bocce courts where you can stake the check on a little friendly competition.

SOLBAR

755 Silverado Trail
Southeast of Lake County
Highway, at the Solage
Calistoga Resort

Tel. 866.942.7442,
solagecalistoga.com

Open daily 7 a.m. to 3 p.m.
and 5 p.m. to 11 p.m.

CALISTOGA SPA HOT SPRINGS

1006 Washington Street
North on Lake County Avenue
from Highway 29, east on
Washington Street

Tel 707.942.6269,
calistogaspa.com

Open daily 10 a.m. to 9 p.m.

CALISTOGA IS Napa Valley's ultimate hot spot. For more than a century, this small town on the northern end of the tasting trail has been famous for its natural hot springs, and the area is dotted with resorts and spas offering mud baths, beauty treatments, and long soaks in the mineral pools. While there are many spas to choose from at the northern end of the Napa Valley, Calistoga Spa Hot Springs is the place the locals come, especially in the evenings after 7 p.m. when the price is reduced to just $15 (day passes $25). Four large pools are naturally heated to different temperatures, and folks bring picnics and bottles of wine to share at the tables. On long summer nights, you can lounge poolside with a book or just take in the atmosphere. Massage and spa treatments are available by appointment, and the guest rooms are recently renovated as well, which is welcome news for wine country visitors. Be sure to come early for a day pass during the peak summer season; the visitor day passes are limited and often not offered on weekends and holidays from Memorial Day to Labor Day.

I CAN NEVER DECIDE which I like better, the hot springs at the Calistoga Spa or the luxurious pools at Indian Springs, so the best recommendation is to try both. Of the two, Indian Springs is a bit more posh—although by Napa standards this is still very much a down-to-earth kind of place. Driving into the resort, you'll begin to wonder if you've stepped back a bit into time, when California was still old Hollywood and everything was just a bit more glamorous.

INDIAN SPRINGS RESORT

**1712 Lincoln Avenue
North on Lake County Avenue
from Highway 29**

Tel. 707.942.4913,
indianspringscalistoga.com

Open daily 9 a.m. to 8 p.m.

There is just one mineral pool, dating to 1917, but it is large and spacious. You can easily spend a day paddling about, tanning poolside, and drinking the signature cucumber water. The resort no longer offers day passes to the pools—to the great distress of many dedicated locals—but if you're looking for a place to stay on your trip to the Napa Valley, Indian Springs is a great choice. Or book a day-spa treatment and take advantage of the chance for a long soak: they offer a full range of indulgences, including mud baths and massage. Excellent winter packages extend tempting discounts.

CHAPTER 4

HOWELL MOUNTAIN

WINERIES

Maps on pages viii–ix

ON THE NORTHEASTERN SLOPES of the Napa Valley, rising above the low fogs that often settle along the valley floor, the vineyards on Howell Mountain are often blessed with several extra hours of sunlight, and the resulting grapes ripen to physiological maturity in a cool mountain climate. These wines show the same kind of stark beauty that you can see all around you in the area's wildly rugged landscape.

Visiting the small wineries on the back roads of Howell Mountain is a delightful way to spend a day in the wine country—and you might as well plan to spend the day. These are places well off the beaten path, and it can take half an hour or more to reach some of them after you leave the Silverado Trail. The best advice is to plan ahead and schedule two or three wine tasting appointments on the mountain and bring a picnic hamper. There are no restaurants up here, and both gourmet supplies and gasoline are limited in Angwin, the last little village on the route up the hillside.

CIMAROSSA

Directions provided with
appointment

Tel. 707.307.3130,
cimarossa.com

Vineyard tour by
appointment only

IN ITALIAN, *cimarossa* means "red hilltop," and the red volcanic soil up here on Howell Mountain inspired the Italian-born owner, Dino Dina, and his wife, Corry Dekker, to give the name to their vineyard. Dino grew up in Genoa and spent summers on a farm. When he and Corry bought this property back in the 1990s, it was a horse ranch and not a winery. They quickly realized that this was great terroir though, and today the estate is planted to Cabernet Sauvignon and to the Italian varietal Nebbiolo. They produce one blend and three single-vineyard-designate wines (ranging from $65 for the blend to $85 for the vineyard designates).

One of the reasons the wines here are so special is that the grapes are grown on a high valley knoll, and the elevations range from seventeen hundred to twenty-one hundred feet above sea level. That means that the tour is not just back lane but back-country: you'll jump in a red Polaris Ranger and loop around the property for an up-close view of the vineyard blocks and wind up at a small wood cabin with some great views. If you're lucky, Dino will have just cooked up some homemade bread, which you can sample alongside the estate olive oil they also make at Cimarossa.

Vineyard tours ($45) are limited, and if you try to find the address using a GPS you will get hopelessly lost, so to visit call or send a request on the website. They would be delighted to welcome you and will tell you the easy way to find them.

BLUE HALL VINEYARD

Directions provided with
appointment

Tel. 888.700.4114,
bluehallvineyard.com

Tasting by appointment only

SEVENTEEN HUNDRED feet up, in the Howell Mountain AVA, visitors to the wine country will also find Blue Hall Vineyard, nestled among the pine and oak forest. The vineyards were planted in 2000 by Andrew Zolopa—a renowned HIV researcher, whose day job is as a professor of medicine at Stanford University—and his wife, Annie Talbot, also a physician at Stanford and the University of Montreal. The name of the winery is a nod to a quotation by author Robert Louis Stevenson, who spent his honeymoon on Howell Mountain in 1880 and aptly observed that the quality of the skies up here, far above the Napa Valley floor, is like entering "the blue hall of heaven."

This small family vineyard of just three acres is planted to the Cabernet Sauvignon that has made Howell Mountain famous, and they make just one wine from the property—an estate Cabernet ($75) they call Camiana, after daughters Camille and Juliana. The consulting winemaker is Ted Osborne (page 86), and the wine has already found a strong following and garnered excellent scores in the 90s by *Wine Enthusiast*. Howell Mountain is known for the purity and intensity of the fruit, and this Cabernet is something special.

When you come for a visit, the relaxed tasting takes place on a rustic picnic table under a large old oak tree right in the middle of the vineyards. There are long views of the hills and forests. And, of course, there are even longer views of the blue skies above you. The tasting fee of $50 per person is waived with purchase of wine.

POSSIBLY THE SMALLEST commercial estate vineyard and winery in the Napa Valley, Wise Acre Vineyard is the special project of Lynn and Kirk Grace. Production is under a hundred cases a year—sometimes significantly. After all, the estate is just a half acre, and all of it is hand-farmed with sustainable practices to produce just one wine, a premium Cabernet Sauvignon. Thirty years ago it was Kirk and a few others who pioneered the practice of organic and biodynamic farming in the Napa Valley.

WISE ACRE VINEYARD

Directions provided with appointment

wise.acre@me.com,
wiseacrevineyard.com

Private sales by
appointment only

Lynn and Kirk both come from wine-growing families. Lynn's family owned a small ranch in Oakville, and she grew up working in the vineyards in the Napa Valley. Kirk's folks founded Grace Family Vineyards over in St. Helena, and he's the director of vineyard operations at one of the celebrated large estates in the area, Stag's Leap Wine Cellars.

Their tiny estate is planted to all Cabernet Sauvignon, and the grapes have a great pedigree. The selection of budwood is from Grace Family Vineyard and is something of a legend in the valley. Wines are available only in three-bottle allocations (for $450), and there isn't a public tasting room or a tour. But if you're interested in picking up something special for your cellar that you won't find anywhere back home, get in touch to ask if they can accommodate. You may get a chance to visit and hear about their personal farm story. Either way, they are delighted to add you to their mailing list if you want to learn about new releases and allocations.

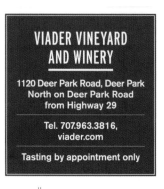

VIADER VINEYARD AND WINERY

1120 Deer Park Road, Deer Park
North on Deer Park Road
from Highway 29

Tel. 707.963.3816,
viader.com

Tasting by appointment only

DELIA VIADER (pronounced vee-ah-dare) grew up in France as the daughter of a diplomat and might never have become a winemaker at all, having completed a doctorate in philosophy at the Sorbonne and studied financial management at M.I.T. and the University of California, Berkeley. But she was a wine enthusiast—and, as a single mother, she wanted to raise her children in a place like Napa.

When she founded Viader in the mid-1980s, after the heyday of the 1970s and before the renaissance of the 1990s, there wasn't a lot of glamour in the California wine business, and there were only a handful of women working as vignerons. Delia started out making fewer than fifteen hundred cases a year. She came to the winemaking business with a global perspective, and from the beginning her wines have found their place among the great vintages of the world. Today Delia runs the winery with the help of her son, Alan, who has been the full-time winemaker since the 2006 vintage, and her daughter, Janet, who is on the sales and marketing side of the enterprise. Together, they produce around seven thousand cases annually, and the Viader wines have been among *Wine Spectator*'s Top 100 Wines on several occasions—including the number one spot on the publication's cover for the 1999 vintage.

Despite having earned a place on the world stage, this is a word-of-mouth winery. Delia makes wines, she says, for a global palate, and the proof is in the tasting. The Viader wines aren't made in the style of the California "fruit bomb," where the rich fruit and berry flavors take precedence over some of a wine's more subtle structural elements. The estate is best known for its super premium Viader Cabernet Sauvignon and Cabernet Franc blend ($115), although it also produces a clonal blend of Syrah and a Cabernet Sauvignon (blended with just a pinch of Malbec) that they call Viader Black Label ($65). Under the "V" label there is an expressive Petit Verdot and Cabernet Sauvignon blend ($125), and the winery bottles as "Dare" wines a changing lineup of more experimental releases—a Tempranillo, a 100 percent Cabernet Franc, and a summer rosé of Cabernet Sauvignon that always sells out within a matter of weeks ($25 to $50).

The other winemakers in the valley will tell you that the view from the back deck of the tasting room at Viader is easily one of the most spectacular in all of Napa, and there are few spots anywhere more perfectly suited for watching the sunset over the hills of the wine country. The Mayacamas range and Mount St. Helena are spread out before you, the welcome is gracious, and the wines delicious no matter what time of the day you come. There are significant discounts for purchases on the futures program (30 percent) and the Viader wine club (15 percent). The fee for tasting is $50, waived with purchase.

LADERA VINEYARDS

150 White Cottage Road
South, Angwin
North on Deer Park Road from
Highway 29 or 121, north on
White Cottage Road

Tel. 707.965.2445,
laderavineyards.com

Tasting by appointment only

AGWIN IS A LONG WAY above the valley floor, and if you're planning a visit to the famed hillside vineyards on Howell Mountain—Napa's first recognized subappellation—spending the day makes the most sense. There are more than a dozen small vintners clustered around White Cottage Road and Summit Lake Drive, and one you wouldn't want to miss is Ladera Vineyards. This mountain terroir was first planted to Zinfandel as early as the 1870s, and the stone winery on the property dates back to the 1880s. The first proprietors delivered their grapes by carriage to Oakville, sending long-distance messages by lantern from nearby Sentinel Hill.

When owners Anne and Pat Stotesbery set about restoring the winery in early 2000, the old wood floors were remilled and used as paneling in the open barn-style tasting room and production facility. Today, there are eighty-one acres of planted vineyards on the property, and the family business—run by Anne and Pat, with the help of three of their four children—produces a range of excellent wines, including a Howell Mountain designate Sauvignon Blanc. There is also a Howell Mountain 100 percent Merlot, a Howell Mountain Cabernet, and one of the rare 100 percent Malbec wines in California (prices from around $30 to $100).

Pat and Anne started out cattle ranching in Montana and came to Napa to pursue their passion for wines. Wine-club members are invited to use the winery's caves for private dinners and special events, and they offer a unique hands-on harvest experience for anyone hankering to experience his or her first crush. It's a chance to participate in one of the most festive times of the year and get a deluxe behind-the-scenes look at what making premium wine is all about (prices from $1,200). There are also occasional twilight winery tours, where you can enjoy the beautiful gardens at dusk and soak up the atmosphere at one of the valley's most picturesque ghost wineries (page 118). The charge for tasting is $15; the tasting and complete winery tour is $50; the fee is often waived with a significant purchase of wine.

GHOST WINERIES

Napa's modern reputation as a premium wine region dates from the 1970s, when a small group of pioneering vintners made their way onto the world stage with wines that started winning some of the industry's most prestigious tasting contests. This was not a new development in the county, however. It was a return to a winemaking tradition that had flourished in Napa more than a hundred years earlier. By the 1860s, the Napa Valley was renowned as a grape-growing region, and the wines made here were exported around the world. By the early twentieth century, it was already a tourist destination. Then came Prohibition, which stymied the flourishing winemaking culture and stalled the local economic engine for a generation. Vineyards were pulled up and replanted with fruit orchards. Wineries went out of business, and the buildings were turned into hay barns, left abandoned, or sometimes stealthily burnt to the ground for insurance money. Winemaking in much of Napa was on hold until the renaissance of the 1970s.

But not all the vineyards were destroyed. A small proportion of those early plantings survived on family ranches, and today a handful of producers offer "old vine" wines made from pre-Prohibition vineyards. Not all the wineries fell to ruin, either. Those that survived are known as "ghost wineries." Sometimes they are abandoned properties in the midst of vineyards, where you can take a twilight tour and experience shades of old Napa. Sometimes they have been converted to new uses. Increasingly, the ghost wineries are being restored to active production, largely due to local efforts in historic preservation and a licensing regulation that makes the expensive and complicated process of bonding a winery in the valley vastly simpler for any owner who can prove that a historic winemaking facility once existed on the property. Today, there are several dozen active ghost wineries in the Napa Valley, each with a storied past, and there are likely to be more in the decades to come.

LAMBORN FAMILY VINEYARDS

1984 Summit Lake Drive, Angwin
North on Deer Park Road from Highway 29 or 121, north on White Cottage Road, west on Summit Lake Drive

Tel. 925.254.0511, lamborn.com

Tours by appointment only

HERE IN NAPA, there are back lane wineries, and then there are back lane wineries. If you are looking for the unfiltered experience of family winemaking—the kind of place where you stand on the summit of a mountain vineyard with the world at your feet and get your shoes muddy walking through the vines with a winegrower—then Lamborn should be at the top of your list. Perched high up on Napa's famed Howell Mountain, more than two thousand feet above sea level, the winery offers sweeping views of pine forests and far canyons, where growers occasionally have to contend with the bears who stop by to eat the fruit off the vines at harvest.

Now in its third generation, the winery was founded in the early 1970s by the father-and-son team of Bob and Mike Lamborn, who started out selling grapes from the hillside property and making some garage wine that Mike admits was pretty dubious. But the fault was never with the grapes, and this is some of the most coveted terroir in the valley. By 1983, the family had released their first commercial vintage. In 1996, Heidi Barrett—the winemaker behind the super cult vintages at Screaming Eagle—began crafting the Lamborn wines, and, today, Mike and his wife, Terry, run the ten-acre estate vineyards with sons Matt and Brian.

Mountain wines in the Napa Valley are known for their beautiful tannins, the combined result of cooler days and, here above the fog line, more hours of sunshine. The grapes ripen slowly. These aren't fruit–bomb wines but vintages that will age beautifully, an increasingly rare thing in the wine country when it comes to Zinfandel, which is one of the two wines in the Lamborn portfolio ($45). Of course, they also make a hillside Cabernet ($115). These are the wines that made Napa famous, and, with a total annual production of fewer than two thousand cases, the Lamborn wines are in demand. If you want to sample them, a visit to this mountaintop vineyard is your best bet. Bring a pair of good walking shoes and all those agricultural questions you always wanted to ask a winegrower. Appointments need to be made several weeks in advance.

SUMMIT LAKE
VINEYARDS AND WINERY

2000 Summit Lake Drive,
Angwin
North on Deer Park Road from
Highway 29 or 121, north on
White Cottage Road, west on
Summit Lake Drive

Tel. 707.965.2488,
summitlakevineyards.com

Tasting by appointment only

FEW THINGS ARE MORE characteristically Napa than sipping a glass of something special out in the vineyards and dreaming a bit about what life might be like in the wine country. And there are few places more beautiful to do that bit of dreaming than up on the top of Howell Mountain. Among the places not to miss here far above the valley floor is Summit Lake Vineyards and Winery, which has been owned and operated by the Brakesman family since the early 1970s.

When the family bought the land, growing on it were some pre-Prohibition Zinfandel vines that had been abandoned for more than thirty years, and the initial plan was to fix up the vineyards and flip the property. As it turns out, the Brakesmans never left. Family and friends helped replant the vineyards, and by the late 1980s the estate was producing a couple hundred cases of wine a year.

Today, production caps out at just over a thousand cases annually, and, in addition to a Zinfandel and a Zinfandel port, there are small lots of hillside Cabernet Sauvignon and Petite

Sirah (wines from around $20 to $65). All the wines are named for grandchildren. This is a word-of-mouth kind of winery—they don't submit their wines to contests and don't advertise. Instead, the family encourages folks to educate their own palate, to discover what they like in a wine and why. The wines produced here on Howell Mountain—some of the most coveted vineyard property in the valley—have expressive tannins and a unique minerality that's hard not to love.

On warm days, tasting at Summit Lake takes place outside, where you can enjoy the views of Pope Valley and the Yolo Mountains in the distance. On rainy days, you'll gather around the kitchen table. If you're traveling with children, the barnyard ducks and farm animals will be an instant hit, and you're welcome to bring a picnic up from the valley if you're planning to spend the day on the mountain. The $15 tasting fee is applied toward your purchase.

A PASSIONATE LOVE of wine led Joyce Black Sears and Jerre Sears to purchase this rural property up on Howell Mountain in 1980, and, without any fanfare or big advertising budget, they have been quietly making about eight hundred cases of mountain wines from some of the finest fruit raised in their vineyards. While most of the grapes are sold to prestigious winemakers throughout the valley, Joyce and Jerre—along with their daughter, Ashley, and son-in-law, Chris—reserve some of their annual crop to make a couple of wines each year under their own label. The idea behind estate wines is to make something that captures the essence of place, and that's the focus at Black Sears, where the flagship wines are a Zinfandel ($50), a Cabernet Sauvignon ($80), and a Cabernet Franc ($85), all 100 percent varietal, with the intense tannins and complex aromas that have made this one of the most coveted appellations in Napa.

Visits to the Howell Mountain estate are limited, and this remote location is beyond back lane. These are wines made amid some of the wine country's most rugged splendor, and they are categorically wines you are not going to find anywhere back home.

CLARK-CLAUDON VINEYARDS

P.O. Box 15, St. Helena
Tasting off-site; call for details

Tel. 707.965.9393,
clarkclaudon.com

Tasting by appointment only

LAND COSTS A FORTUNE in the Napa Valley, so it takes some special magic for a young couple to be able to purchase 154 acres of hillside property on Howell Mountain. When Laurie Clark-Claudon tells the story of how she and her husband, Tom, were able to make a life for themselves in the wine country, she puts it down to hard work, a willingness to take a risk, serendipity, and the kindness of strangers.

In the 1980s, Tom started his own vineyard management company and was tending the grapes for prestigious clients like Spottswoode and St. Supéry, while Laurie worked as a schoolteacher and then a psychotherapist. When a friend told them about a property for sale up in the hills above the Napa Valley, they went to have a look and fell in love with the place, but the price was completely beyond their reach. To their astonishment, the owner worked with them over a period of years to make sure they could buy it.

Today, this special piece of the wine country is home to the Clark-Claudon Vineyards, where their estate Cabernet Sauvignon wines are born. The vineyards are run by Tom and Laurie; their children, Briana and Josh, and their spouses. They are occasionally assisted, of course, by the young third generation, who are learning to pick leaves out of the bins at harvest. Wine tasting ($50 per person, waived with purchase of three or more bottles) takes place in a small cottage where the views from the deck take in the vineyards and creek and the forest beyond, and guests settle in with wine and cheese to savor the mountain here at nearly a thousand feet above the valley floor. You can also sample their wines at the Vintner's Collective, 1245 Main Street, Napa (vintnerscollective.com).

Eighteen acres are planted to vineyards, and the property is a natural oasis for bears, coyote, birds, and even the occasional mountain lion. The Clark-Claudon Wild Iris Sauvignon Blanc (around $30), made with fruit from vineyards farmed by Josh and his company, Clark Vineyard Management, is named for the flowers that grow at the edge of the estate vineyard. The label of their estate Cabernet Sauvignon (around $85), an elegant wine with luscious mountain tannins, features the winery's signature feathers, a nod to the wildlife that surrounds them here on Howell Mountain. Occasionally, a wine made from the thousand vines planted around the family home is released under their Eternity label ($125). These are small-production lots (under fifteen hundred cases) from one of Napa's most prestigious appellations, and those who know the Clark-Claudon wines won't be surprised to learn that, since their first release in 1993, they have received scores in the 90s for every single vintage produced.

this world famous
ving region

VALLEY

napa valley vintners

...and
the wine
is bottled
poetry...

CHAPTER 5
SPRING MOUNTAIN

WINERIES

Maps on pages viii–ix

LOCATED UP IN THE STEEP HILLS that rise above the western floor of the Napa Valley and connect California's most celebrated wine country with its prestigious neighbor in Sonoma, the Spring Mountain District is one of the most beautiful parts of a beautiful place. The thirty-odd wineries in the appellation are mostly strung out along Spring Mountain Road, which twists and turns its way dramatically through small wooded canyons up to a high natural pass. The road then begins its descent into Sonoma County.

The Spring Mountain District has only about a thousand acres of vineyards, and this is a place where few tourists come. The tasting experiences on the mountain—where small family wineries and hand-tilled vineyards are the norm—are wonderfully intimate, and the wines from the appellation are among the world's most coveted. Because of the distance from the main tasting route, this is a place to spend a day, bringing along an al fresco luncheon or making plans for a catered meal at one of the wineries.

THE DRY-FARMED estate vineyards at Smith-Madrone bear the traces of a historical development in the wine country. The vineyard was first established in the 1880s and then abandoned with the onset of the phylloxera infection that decimated grape crops around the world at the beginning of the twentieth century. In the sixty-odd years that followed, the forest reclaimed the abandoned vineyard land.

In 1971 Stuart Smith founded Smith-Madrone and, with his brother Charlie, cleared the forest, replanted the vineyards, and built the winery. Visitors can still see rows of ancient olive trees that date back to the original vineyards—and abundant evidence of the madrone trees that made up the second part of the name the Smith family has given to their hillside winery.

Today, four decades later, the two still grow the grapes, make the wine, and conduct the tastings with visitors. The family's focus is on making old-fashioned Napa Valley wines that are distinctive, express the vintage, and balanced and complex. The Smith-Madrone Cabernet Sauvignon was recently singled out as "my desert island Napa Valley Cabernet" by *New York Times* wine writer Eric Asimov. If you're in the mood for something even more special than that, the winery introduced in 2012 its first reserve wine. They also make Riesling and Chardonnay wines. Wines range from around $30 to $200.

Here on this mountaintop family vineyard there is no charge for the tastings, which are always led by one of the Smith brothers.

RELIC WINES

4078 Spring Mountain Road,
St. Helena
Exit Madrona Avenue
southwest from
Highway 29, west on Spring
Mountain Road

Tel. 707.967.9380,
relicwines.com

Tasting by appointment only

RELIC WINES is the small artisanal project of the husband-and-wife team of winemaker Michael Hirby and Schatzi Throckmorton. Michael has a great reputation in the valley as the consulting winemaker at a number of prestigious estates, and Schatzi is the longtime general manager at Behrens Family Winery. That's part of the reason the couple hosts their tastings at the Behrens Family estate (page 152), while their own new winery and tasting room on Soda Canyon Road is under construction (so check their website for the new address after late 2014).

At Relic, they are doing something interesting and special: after some research into the ancient winemaking techniques in the Rhône, Burgundy, and Bordeaux, they came up with the idea of trying those old secrets out on great fruit from the Napa Valley and Sonoma Coast AVAs. The result is a miniscule but highly collectible production of Pinot Noir and Chardonnay wines that don't taste quite like anything else in California. The critics have already taken notice. The wines range from $45 to $90, and most of the production is presold by allocation, but, if you want a chance to try something rare and to get on the list, there are hillside private tastings ($25) where new enthusiasts are warmly welcomed.

MARSTON FAMILY VINEYARD

P.O. Box 668, St. Helena
Tasting off-site; call for details

Tel. 707.963.8490,
marstonfamilyvineyard.com

Vineyard tour and tasting
by appointment only

SOMETIMES IN the wine country there are places so beautiful that you can't quite believe you've stumbled upon them, and among all my Napa Valley picks—and there are some stunningly wonderful places—the Marston Family Vineyard is right at the very top of the charts. These are great wines, created in the midst of splendor and history and made by some of the nicest people you'll ever meet.

It's a long and winding drive up to the estate, past hot springs and riverbeds and redwood forests, and then you'll turn up a small track where the view opens onto hillside vineyards and distant views of tree-covered mountain slopes. Of the original five hundred acres that the Marston family purchased back in the 1960s as a summer retreat, almost half have been donated to the Land Trust of Napa County, an organization devoted to preserving the wild rural spaces of the wine country. The result is a woodland oasis, where wild turkeys meander through the vineyards and where you feel a thousand miles away from the frantic tourist pace of St. Helena on a summer day.

At eleven hundred feet, these are steep hillside vineyards that produce the rich mountain tannins that have made the Napa Valley famous. Winemakers here use gentle barrel fermentation to tame those tannins without jeopardizing the complex layering of the fruits. Of the fifty acres of vineyards on the property, the oldest were planted back in the 1920s using horse and plow, and, while there are a few historic blocks, most of the family's vineyards were replanted in the 1990s to Cabernet Sauvignon, Merlot, and Syrah.

The Marstons make just two wines a year—a terrific 100 percent estate Cabernet Sauvignon ($115), which *Wine News* has ranked as its number one publisher's pick and awarded a stellar 96 points, and a beautiful Sauvignon Blanc–led proprietary blend they call Albion in tribute to family roots in England ($50). It's the first white wine the family has made since the 1980s.

Three generations of Marstons run the family winery—parents Michael and Alexandra, children Elizabeth and John, their spouses Jamie and Tanya, and a senior generation of Marston grandparents. The tasting room is a vintage tin-roofed hay barn, once the site of an old ghost winery on the property, with the feel of a New England 1920s summer camp. One of the property's many natural springs bubbles up in the courtyard, and just beyond you can see the old track of the original stagecoach road that once ran past the barn and connected this most southerly end of Spring Mountain to the higher elevations and then to Sonoma County on the far side of the valley. When you visit, be sure to ask to see the sign that Clark Gable—who spent his honeymoon in the cottage on the property—once used for target practice, and make sure you also learn about the Marston second label E. J. It's a small project that the younger Elizabeth and John have recently started, representing the best in the next generation of Napa winemaking.

SPRING MOUNTAIN is one of Napa Valley's most scenic appellations, and, although this AVA has been making some of America's most acclaimed wines for decades, visitors to the wine country have only recently discovered the scenic tasting rooms tucked away here in the hills that separate Napa from Sonoma County. One of the pioneers in making world-class wines on Spring Mountain is Robert Keenan Winery, founded on the site of an old nineteenth-century ghost winery in the 1970s by Robert Keenan and still run today by his son, Michael.

For Robert Keenan, a life in the wine business was the natural outgrowth of his passion for the history of the great French châteaux—and his gift for real estate investment. Because his maternal grandfather was an avid collector of fine French wines, Michael grew up appreciating great vintages. Today the winery produces some great vintages of its own. This was one of *Wine and Spirit*'s top 100 wineries of the year in 2006, and, since 2001, forty-seven of its wines have received scores of 90 points or more from critic Robert Parker, including the 97-point 2008 Cabernet Sauvignon reserve. Among the white wines, there is a standout summer blend of Chardonnay, Viognier, and Marsanne, and, Michael will tell you with a laugh, "We also do a nonmalolactic Chardonnay, so it actually doesn't suck." It's an impressive record for a fifty-acre estate whose total annual production is under fifteen thousand cases a year.

Unusually in the valley, the family was able to restore the original Italian hill-style winery, and the drive up Spring Mountain road is easily one of the most beautiful rural routes in the wine country. Most wines are in the $25 to $100 range, and there is a $20 fee for tasting appointments.

WHEN ANGUS AND MARGARET Wurtele bought this vineyard estate on Spring Mountain in the 1990s, it might as well have been Sleeping Beauty's castle. Originally built in the 1970s as the site of the Yverdon Winery, the vineyards had been torn out and the building shuttered for more than a decade. The hillside terrain was so overgrown that it meant hacking a pathway to the doorstep.

Today, renamed Terra Valentine—a nod to Angus's father who was born on February 14 and built a commercial empire in the varnish business—the estate looks every bit the fairytale retreat. Perched a thousand feet above the valley floor, amid great natural beauty, the château-style stone winery is illuminated with the original stained glass windows depicting themes from classical literature and winemaking. The deluxe two-and-a-half-hour tasting appointment (starting at $45), which focuses on wine education and pairs the Terra Valentine wines with artisanal cheeses and dark chocolate, takes place under the watchful eye of St. Geneviève de Paris, in a room decorated with eighteenth-century English oak panels originally destined for the Hearst Castle in San Simeon. There is also a winery tour and tasting experience ($45), a chance to try what wine aficionados call a "vertical" (a tasting of the same wine over a series of successive vintages and a great way to learn why vintage matters) for around $60, and the opportunity to arrange an even more exclusive private visit. Be sure to call ahead or check their website, because not all the experiences are offered every day.

The winery has two estate vineyards, one here on the property and one a bit farther down the valley, and the real emphasis is on Cabernet Sauvignon wines. There is also an estate Syrah, a dry Alsatian-style Riesling, a late-harvest Riesling, a beautiful French-style Pinot Noir from Sonoma, a full-bodied Bordeaux blend, and a summer rosé (most wines from $30 to $65, some reserve wines higher). The winemaker is the very talented Sam Baxter. Tasting fees are applied to the purchase of several bottles.

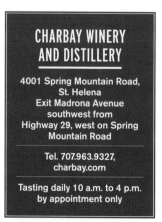

CHARBAY WINERY AND DISTILLERY

4001 Spring Mountain Road, St. Helena
Exit Madrona Avenue southwest from Highway 29, west on Spring Mountain Road

Tel. 707.963.9327, charbay.com

Tasting daily 10 a.m. to 4 p.m. by appointment only

RUN BY TWO GENERATIONS of the Karakasevic family, Charbay has a reputation as one of the finest producers of boutique spirits in the country, and outside their Napa Valley still house and winery you can get what might be your first look at an Alambic Charentais pot still. Theirs originally came from Cognac, France. Miles is from Serbia and is a twelfth-generation Grand Master Distiller. Son Marko, generation thirteen to carry on the family craft, is now a Master Distiller after a grueling apprenticeship under his father. They take the title very seriously here. *Spirit Journal* has ranked Charbay's vodka the best in the world for several years running, and the distillery's limited-release whiskey ($350) is a runaway cult favorite.

What fewer people know is that the family has been making wines, brandy, and aperitifs up on their Spring Mountain estate—at twenty-three hundred feet above sea level, the highest tasting bar in the county—for more than twenty-five years. They produce a variety of wines, including around sixty cases a year of Chardonnay, maybe a hundred cases of dry rosé, and of course a 100 percent Cabernet Sauvignon wine made from fruit grown in Oakville (wines from $25 to

$50). You'll also find a range of ports, fruit wines, and wine-based aperitifs. Poured over ice, these aperitifs are perfect summer afternoon cocktails. They're made with the brandy the family distills.

The tasting room is set along a rural back road above the Napa Valley, and, in the winter months, when the still is running, it's a cozy and relaxed place to try something just a little bit different. The distillery and winery are then filled with the scent of wood barrels, and visitors sample the wines, ports, and aperitifs (tasting $20). Cigars are available for an al fresco port and cigar pairing. And, while California law won't allow you to taste any of the stronger stuff here at the tasting room, the family offers a terrific seminar on the art of distilling, taught by folks who are unquestionably masters ($40). They are true craftsmen. Marko's wife, Jenni, and baby, Miles, are often seen at events these days, making this a family affair you'll remember.

PRIDE MOUNTAIN VINEYARDS

4026 Spring Mountain Road,
St. Helena
Exit Madrona Avenue
southwest from Highway 29,
west on Spring Mountain
Road, north on Summit Trail

Tel. 707.963.4949,
pridewines.com

Tasting by appointment only;
closed Tuesday

THE OLD STAGECOACH ROAD from St. Helena to Santa Rosa once ran across Spring Mountain in the days before there was a county line separating Sonoma on the west from Napa on the east. Down in the Pride Mountain vineyards, the ruins of an old stone arch still mark the route of this first wine country highway, and today the county line runs right through the middle of the family estate. In fact, in order to meet the strict regulations that govern the production and appellation of wines in Northern California, the Pride family spends some of their time during the crush moving equipment from one side of that line to the other.

What this means is that, perhaps uniquely, Pride Mountain Vineyards produces both Sonoma and Napa wines made from a single ranch, and, if you ever wanted to learn about the complex intersection of terroir and appellation in winemaking, there is no better place to get a firsthand introduction. There is also no better place to learn about the world-class wines both counties have to offer either.

Pride Mountain Vineyards is owned and operated by the brother-and-sister team of Steve Pride and Suzanne Pride Bryan, with founder and mother Carolyn Pride still taking an interest. When the family bought the ranch back in 1989, the first "tasting room" was a board between two barrels. Now, visitors gather around a pewter bar in an art-filled foyer, where the atmosphere is friendly and welcoming.

The Pride wines have made *Wine Spectator*'s top 100 wines list on five occasions, including the 2005 Reserve Cabernet Sauvignon and the 2007 Merlot, and Robert Parker of *Wine Advocate* has tapped the winery as one of the top in the world. These wines have been served at the White House more than twenty-five times—by four different administrations.

The fee for tasting is $15 per person. If at all possible, get a spot at the 10 a.m. tasting—it's the only appointment of the day that includes the vineyard tour ($20).

You are also welcome to stop off on your own at the nineteenth-century stone ruins of the old Summit Winery, located on the Pride Mountain property. Legend has it that the winery was burned down during Prohibition for the insurance money, and it's a hauntingly picturesque spot.

If you're touring the wine country with more than a few friends, there is a private tasting room with seating up to a dozen people, where you can sit down for a more focused and educational experience ($20). Pride also offers an exclusive private tasting in the caves for special occasions ($75).

Pride Mountain Vineyards is renowned for its signature Cabernet Sauvignon wines and produces excellent wines from other varietals grown on the property, including a Merlot, Sangiovese, Chardonnay, Viognier, and Syrah, and a very small production dessert wine, Mistelle de Viognier. Prices range from $40 to $135, with most wines in the $60 range.

ERNA SCHEIN

BEHRENS FAMILY
WINERY

4078

BEHRENS & HITCHCOCK

←

— 4054

B

If you want to understand why Napa Valley has a reputation for world-class wines—and, in the bargain, you want to see some of the most gorgeous scenery going—Barnett Vineyards is a must. There are tours of the working winery and a chance to taste these small-production wines in an intimate and friendly setting. The fee for tasting is $40 for current vintages and $65 for library tastings.

BEHRENS FAMILY WINERY

4078 Spring Mountain Road,
St. Helena
Exit Madrona Avenue
southwest from
Highway 29, west on Spring
Mountain Road

Tel. 707.963.1774,
behrensfamilywinery.com

Tasting by appointment only

LES BEHRENS and Lisa Drinkward started making wines up in California's northern Humboldt County back in the early 1990s, when they had the idea to buy some grapes and make some house wine to serve at the award-winning restaurant they owned and ran. When it turned out they had a knack for making great wines, they found themselves with a growing project and, before too long, with a dilemma. They realized they would either have to run a restaurant or run a winery because there just weren't enough hours in a day to do both.

So the winery was born. In 1997, they sold the restaurant, and the next year, with partner Bob Hitchcock, they purchased a piece of hilltop winery property in Napa's Spring Mountain District. Although Bob retired back in 2004, Les and Lisa still make one wine under the Behrens & Hitchcock label, a Cabernet Sauvignon they dub "The Heavyweight," which earned 93 points from Robert Parker for one recent vintage. The majority of their three thousand cases a year are produced under the name Behrens Family Winery. There have been rave reviews, but Les will tell you that it's actually all about a winemaker putting heart and soul into a bottle. That's what you can taste in a really great wine.

The California wine country is filled with gorgeous views and natural beauty that will sometimes leave you breathless, but these little wineries up on Spring Mountain are some of Napa's most stunning. In the afternoons, there is a luminous quality to the atmosphere and long views over forested valleys. Tasting at Behrens Family Winery takes place amid all this splendor, in a vintage, wood-paneled Westcraft trailer, where there are quirky old postcards with scenes of the wine country and a window view.

There are five wines under the Behrens Family label, including a Bordeaux blend and other blends working primarily with Petite Sirah, Syrah, and Cabernet Franc varietals. The wines range from $50 to $85 and are currently available only by allocation, but you can always get added to the list if you're an enthusiast. For anyone who thinks that Napa is all glitz and glitter, this is the other side of the county—the kind of place where the pace is relaxed, the people are friendly, and the real work of making wine is the only thing on display.

FISHER VINEYARDS

6200 St. Helena Road,
Santa Rosa
Exit Calistoga Road north
from Highway 12, east from
St. Helena Road

Tel. 707.539.7511,
fishervineyards.com

Tasting by appointment only

FRED AND JUELLE FISHER bought their first hundred acres of vineyard property up on Spring Mountain in 1973, and today they produce five thousand cases of handcrafted wines with both Sonoma County and Napa Valley appellations. While the Spring Mountain tasting room is technically on the western—Sonoma—side of the county line that runs through the Mayacamas range, the family also farms seventy acres of land along the storied Silverado Trail.

Their children grew up in these vineyards on both sides of the county line, and today the winery is a two-generation family affair, with all three of the children involved in daily operations. From the Spring Mountain tasting room, there are views in both directions, as far as the Sonoma Coast to the west and Knight's Valley to the east, and the terraced vineyards glow golden in the late afternoon sun up here in the mountain terroir. The wood for the winery was milled from redwood trees and fir on the property, and, in the warmer months, tasting takes place outdoors where there's a wood-fired pizza oven. There aren't any restaurants up on Spring Mountain, and if you're looking to work a lunch into your tasting itinerary, gourmet spreads can be included as part of a visit ($100 per person).

The winemaker's tour and tasting includes a walk through the vineyards, a trip through the cellars and the working winery, and, of course, the chance to sample some of these premium wines. The Fisher family produces both Sonoma County and Napa Valley single-vineyard-designate Cabernet Sauvignon wines, a range of Bordeaux-style red wines that includes a Napa

Valley Merlot and Cabernet Franc blend, and Syrah and Chardonnay wines made from grapes on the Spring Mountain estate. The Napa Valley Cabernet from the Lamb Vineyard has consistently scored points in the 90s from *Wine Advocate*, and the 1997 Wedding Vineyard Cabernet—described as "potentially perfect" and a "modern-day California legend"—is, at 99 points, one of highest ranking American Cabernets ever made. The fee for tasting is $40, waived with the purchase of three or more bottles.

CHAPTER 6

DOWNTOWN ST. HELENA AND ENVIRONS

WINERIES

PROVISIONS

DIVERSIONS

Maps on pages viii–ix

THE SMALL CITY OF ST. HELENA is arguably the cultural heart of the Napa wine country, and Highway 29 runs right through the middle of its quaint—and often congested—little Main Street. At the peak of the tourist season, driving through downtown St. Helena is an exercise in patience, and perhaps this is the best reason of all to pull over, breathe deeply, and spend a bit of time exploring the area. Here you will find high-end boutiques, art galleries, antique stores, and any number of excellent bistros, restaurants, and wine bars, and it is easy to while away an hour or two in the afternoon wandering the streets and shops. In the morning, before you hit the tasting trail, St. Helena also has several excellent bakeries and cafés, where you can pick up a pastry and a steaming latté on your way to your first appointment. There are many small family wineries tucked in along St. Helena's residential back streets and on the outskirts of the city.

750 WINES

1224 Adams Street,
Downtown St. Helena
Southwest on Adams Street
from Highway 29

Tel. 707.963.0750,
750wines.com

Private tasting by
appointment only

TUCKED DOWN a narrow lane right in the heart of St. Helena is a place that will warm the hearts of serious wine collectors making the trek to the wine country. 750 Wines is a unique wine shop, the brainchild of two Midwestern-born enophiles, Monica and David Stevens, who noticed that there was a need for a top-tier wine merchant that offered not only great wine but also the kind of old-world concierge services that could introduce the premium winemakers to visitors. As they like to joke, they have the wines you want before you know you want them, and their eye for great wines is pretty incredible.

This isn't the kind of place you pop into and jostle for a spot at the tasting room bar. In fact, tasting is by appointment only, and your first meeting takes place at a table in their trendy Tribeca-style loft. If you're looking to develop a long-term relationship, 750 Wines is the answer. They are the conduit in the valley to elite access to cult winemakers and undiscovered superstars; they can help you arrange exclusive experiences and find wines often available only by allocation. The name 750 Wines is a nod to the 750-milliliter size of the standard wine bottle, in a little playful irony—though of course they will tell you with a laugh they will have no trouble finding you a jeroboam of something special if that's your heart's desire.

WHEN YOU'RE PLANNING your day
on the tasting trail, Salvestrin Winery
is one of those places where you want
to leave yourself a bit of extra time. The
people here are so congenial that you
are bound to get chatting, and it would
be a shame to have to cut short something quite so pleasant.

SALVESTRIN WINERY

**397 Main Street
North of the Sulphur Springs
Avenue intersection, look for
the white arches**

Tel. 707.963.5105,
salvestrinwinery.com

Tasting by appointment only

What's hard to believe sometimes
is that this charming winery—which has
nothing of Napa commercial glitz about
it—is hidden right in plain sight, only a
few minutes from downtown St. Helena.
When you arrive, Salvestrin Winery
feels just like what it is: a small family
business and a labor of love. The family has been farming this property since
1932, when John and Emma Salvestrin
bought it from its first recorded owner,
the renowned Napa Valley viticulturalist
Dr. George Crane. Today, three succes-
sive generations of the Salvestrin family are part of the story—
Eddie and Susanne, their son, Rich, and his wife, Shannon, and
their young girls, Tessa, Emma, and Hannah. The senior Salves-
trins live in a sprawling Victorian home next to the vineyards and
tasting room, Rich runs the family business and makes the wines,
and you're likely to meet the big red cat and the two family dogs
in the yard.

While the family has been growing grapes here for more than
seventy-five years, they didn't start commercially producing their
own wines until the mid-1990s, and the winery only opened in

2001. They still sell about half their grapes to other winemakers in the valley. With the rest, they produce around thirty-five hundred cases a year of traditional Italian-style wines and Bordeaux varietals. Coming down the lane to the winery, you drive past their old-vine Sangiovese plantings. Farther back in the vineyards is some Zinfandel that was planted more than a hundred years ago.

If you've always wondered about the significance of old-vine plantings or wanted to ask a winemaker about the history of viticulture in the Napa Valley, there's no better chance. On warm afternoons, wine tasting often starts with a glass of Sauvignon Blanc (around $25 a bottle) on the picnic tables outside the family's small winery, overlooking the vineyards and surrounded by fruit trees. Then, upstairs in the barn, there's a chance to try some of the Salvestrin reds. The estate makes a Cabernet Sauvignon, a Petite Sirah, a 100 percent Sangiovese, a reserve Cabernet Sauvignon, and a signature heritage Italian blend. Called Retaggio, it's a blend of Sangiovese, Merlot, Cabernet Sauvignon, and Petite Sirah. The wines range from $25 to $125, with most around $40, and many are available only in the tasting room or from their allocation list.

The fee for tasting is $25, waived with a purchase of three bottles, and you're welcome to bring a picnic.

WHEN JACK AND MARY NOVAK moved their family to the Napa Valley in 1972, land was still $2,000 an acre and grapes sold at the local co-op for a couple hundred dollars a ton. The plan was to drive a tractor, grow grapes, and maybe make some wine. Jack was a physician, and it seemed like an idyllic place to raise their five children.

As is the way in the wine country, after replanting forty acres of old pre-Prohibition vineyards to Zinfandel, Sauvignon Blanc, and Cabernet Sauvignon and taking classes in viniculture, the family produced, despite Jack's untimely death in 1977, its first vintage of Cabernet Sauvignon in 1982. Named after the historic 1882 Victorian estate and forty-six-acre property that is still the family home, Spottswoode makes, under the stewardship of daughters Beth and Lindy, around six thousand cases a year of acclaimed Cabernet Sauvignon and Sauvignon Blanc wines, the former produced entirely from grapes grown on their organically farmed estate vineyard. *Wine Spectator* lauded Spottswoode's 2009 "beautifully crafted" estate Cabernet as one of the top wines in California and gave it 95 points—but then, points in the 90s and accolades are nothing new at Spottswoode, where the emphasis is on creating world-class wines that will cellar beautifully.

Tasting takes place at a long wooden table in a cheerful ranch house overlooking the historic nineteenth-century stone barn winery that serves as a barrel room and production facility. Wines range from around $40 to $145; there is a $45 charge for tours and tasting.

STEVE AND LINDA GOLDFARB first came to Napa looking for a small weekend place where they could retreat from their busy life in San Francisco as a lawyer and a paralegal. In 1997, they came to the wine country on Linda's birthday and fell in love with a house that happened to come with six rows of grape vines. They moved in over the summer, and, come fall, there were grapes to be picked. The couple went at it with kitchen shears, and eventually their neighbor, a grape grower, took pity on them and suggested hiring some seasoned pickers to help with the small harvest. Using information from every book they could read on home winemaking, Steve and Linda crushed the grapes in their garage and ultimately made thirty cases of wine using a barrel they bought from the folks over at Cakebread Cellars.

Their foray into the winemaking business might have ended there if Linda hadn't happened to be on the board of the local animal shelter. While the wine Steve and Linda made sat in bottles in their garage, Linda worked on the shelter's fundraiser, which included a wine auction. She asked one of the sponsors to put their wine into a blind tasting to see if it were even drinkable. The tasting panel called them the following week and said, "You need to make more of this wine; it's fantastic." And that was how Anomaly Vineyards got its start.

Their first vintage in 1997 was released only to friends. Three years later they hired a winemaker and started commercially producing wines. A new winery soon followed. Anomaly still makes only one wine—a Cabernet Sauvignon blended with a small amount of Petit Verdot and Cabernet Franc ($85). Their vintages consistently receive high praise, but the motto they go by is printed on their cork: "Trust Your Palate."

From the Tuscan-style fieldstone winery, there are impressive views of the Mayacamas Mountains. Tasting appointments take place in the cozy underground cellar. Anomaly also sells a cold-pressed extra-virgin olive oil ($30) imported from Cortona, Italy, where Steve's brother and sister-in-law own a small home on a property with olive orchards; the oils are the fruits of that good fortune. And why is the wine named Anomaly? Steve and Linda will tell you cheerfully that "anomaly" means unusual and unexpected, and "that's us doing this!"

S. E. CHASE FAMILY CELLARS

2252 Sulphur Springs Avenue,
Exit Sulphur Springs Avenue
southwest from Highway 29

Tel. 707.963.1284,
chasecellars.com

Tasting by appointment only,
Wednesday to Saturday

THIS SMALL FAMILY VINEYARD is named after the nineteenth-century rancher Sarah Esther Chase, whose family founded the original Greystone Cellars, today the home of the Culinary Institute of America. Her children planted in 1903 some of the Zinfandel vines that descendants still farm today. Here on this old creek bed, the roots of these dry-farmed plants reach down more than thirty feet to find water, and the result is wine with ripe dark fruits and a large finish. The winery is now run by the brother-and-sister team of Katie and Mike Simpson, the great-great-granddaughter and -grandson of the vineyard founder.

S. E. Chase Family Cellars wines include an old-vine reserve Zinfandel, a Petite Sirah, a Cabernet Sauvignon, and a Sauvignon Blanc (from around $25 to $75). The estate also releases around eighty cases a year of a dry rosé. Readers of *Food & Wine* will have seen the wine featured on the cover of the November 2007 Thanksgiving issue; these are wines that pair well with food.

WINEMAKER DAVID DICKSON
established the winery back in 1978
and named it after his two young sons,
Andrew and Lane. Both boys grew up
here in the wine country, and today
Andrew Lane remains a family business. They produce around seventeen hundred cases a year of premium
wines, focusing on Cabernet Sauvi-

ANDREW LANE WINES

742 Sunnyside Road
Tasting off-site; call for
directions

Tel. 707.815.3501,
andrewlanewines.com

Tasting by appointment only

gnon, Merlot, Petite Sirah, and a great old-fashioned Napa field
blend that is made with primitive and purist "old world" techniques that are hard to find these days. That means the grapes
are fermented whole and unpressed, and this aromatic wine
picks up the flavors of the stems and skins and warm earth.
Most wines are $20 to $50, from fruit sourced around Napa,
Sonoma, and Mendocino.

Son Andrew—known to everyone as Drew—offers intimate
introductions to the art of winemaking in the Napa Valley and
is a one-man wine-education wonder. Drew is also gaining a
national reputation for leading the way in bringing the tradition
of Beaujolais-nouveau-inspired wines—and harvest parties—to
the California wine country. The family recently started making a
small production of "Napa nouveau" from Gamay Noir (around
$20), which they release with much fanfare and merrymaking
during the traditional third week of November.

But the most fun way to taste the Andrew Lanes is to sign
up for Drew's "Surf and Terroir" tour—a stand-up paddleboard
excursion (lesson included) along the Napa River, with wine and
oysters (page 177).

CULINARY INSTITUTE OF AMERICA

**2555 Main Street
Highway 29, just south of
Deer Park Road**

Tel. 707.967.2320,
ciachef.edu/California

Open Tuesday to Saturday
11:30 a.m. to 9 p.m., Sunday
noon to 7:15 p.m.; classes as
announced

ONE OF AMERICA'S most prestigious culinary schools, the Culinary Institute of America—known to aficionados as the CIA—is well known as home to the *Wine Spectator* Greystone Restaurant, where you can watch some of the area's most talented young chefs whip up local delights.

What is less well known—but worth a trip when you are in the wine country—are the one-hour weekend public cooking demonstrations (around $20) in the early afternoon and the wine discovery courses offered at the Rudd Center for Professional Wine Studies (around $100). The wine discovery courses are led by a professional sommelier and focus on introducing passionate enthusiasts to some of the finer points of wine appreciation. If you are ready to get serious about your wine tasting, this is starting at the top. The campus also offers a variety of cooking courses and innovative "boot camps" geared toward home chefs as well as tours of the historical Greystone building, the corkscrew museum, and the culinary herb gardens.

On Sundays in the restaurant there is free corkage from 5 p.m. to close, if you are dying to try your most recent back lane discovery.

LOCATED ALONG Main Street in downtown St. Helena, Cook is the place the local winemakers consider their special joint. And it's easy to see why. The atmosphere here is busy and cheerful, and, on most nights, if you want to try some of Jude Wilmoths's signature braised short ribs with scallion whipped potatoes, advance reservations are a must.

Afternoons are actually my favorite time to stop in for a glass of wine and a plate of homemade pasta at the bar, where I can admire the selection of wines on offer by small family vintners. The pasta dishes are authentic regional Italian delights, and, if you take your espresso to one of the small tables by the window, it's the perfect place to watch this part of the world go by. Most entrées are in the $20 to $25 price range.

This is also the place to try a bottle of the Bressler Vineyards wines, grown just around the corner on a small family vineyard. Their Cabernet Sauvignon, a super-premium and ultra-boutique vintage, typically sells out within a few months of bottling every year, but they also make a food-friendly red wine that pairs perfectly with heartier dishes. Bob and Stacey Bressler—who left careers in high-tech for a life in the wine country—make fewer than five hundred cases a year (bresslervineyards.com).

Jude's local wine list is exceptional, and if you didn't make it out to meet the winemakers, you can try selections from back lane vintners that typically include Failla (page 64), Grassi (page 38), Stony Hill (page 190), Hunnicutt (page 62), Viader (page 114), Venge (page 71), Shafer (page 74), and Anomaly (page 166).

NAPA VALLEY OLIVE MANUFACTURING COMPANY

835 Charter Oak Avenue
Northeast on Charter Oak
Avenue from Highway 29

Tel. 707.963.4173,
oliveoilsainthelena.com

Open Monday to Sunday
9 a.m. to 5 p.m.

IF YOU NEED fixings for a back lane picnic, locals will send you to the Napa Valley Olive Manufacturing Company, which sells some of the wine country's most coveted olive oils and a wide selection of cheeses, provisions, breads, and homemade charcuterie.

The Particelli and Lucchesi families have been doing business out of this roadside barn since the 1930s, and you can find their popular and quirky little shop just down the street from Tra Vigne. Here, your bill is totted up on butcher paper, and the only register is a cash box crammed with crumpled ones and fives. Word on the street is that this place was the original inspiration for the celebrated Oakville Grocery farther down the valley.

BILLED AS a wine country public house, in the short time that Goose & Gander has been open, it has established a reputation as the go-to spot in Napa for creative retro cocktails with a sense of humor. And that is a recipe for hipness. This is where the young wine-makers in the county head after work for a get-together. It's also a great place if you're looking to see what life in the wine country is like after hours. There is live music in the summer on Sunday nights and good food and wine on offer any time they are open. The menu focuses on local ingredients, the bounty of this little sliver of paradise, and American-style small plates and entrées, ranging from updated jalapeño poppers and crispy Pacific oysters to grilled flatiron steak and swordfish (entrées around $15 to $25).

GOOSE & GANDER

**1245 Spring Street
Southwest on Spring Street
from Highway 29**

Tel. 707.967.8779,
goosegander.com

Open daily noon to midnight

THE WHITE BARN

2727 Sulphur Springs Avenue
Exit Sulphur Springs Avenue
southwest from Highway 29

Tel. 707.963.3408,
thewhitebarn.org

Hours based on current
events calendar

THIS 1872 CIVIL WAR-ERA carriage house turned private theater is one of the treasures of the Napa Valley and one taste of the close community ties that the locals nurture in this special corner of the world.

Founded in the 1980s by Nancy Garden, the White Barn epitomizes the North Bay ethos. It's a local playhouse and meeting space where actors, musicians, artists, and writers come to perform—with all proceeds going to support charitable causes both locally and internationally. There are poetry salons and French jazz performances, holiday theatricals and barn dances, community BBQs and picnics, as well music and drama representing a broad range of talent from the Bay Area and beyond.

Complimentary Napa wines are served during the intermissions, donated by vintners from across the region. Performances have benefited everything from the Calistoga community pool to economic opportunities for women in developing countries. The White Barn isn't just about supporting good causes—it's also a charming and beautiful spot where, after a long day on the tasting trail, visitors can enjoy some of the best after-hours entertainment in the area.

NAPA VALLEY, although people often forget it, is a river valley, and the river is an integral part of the geological history of the region. It's also part of the living history and a source of immense natural beauty. If you're looking for a truly unique wine tasting experience, a stand-up paddleboard tour up the Napa River, riding the incoming tide to the Oak Knoll AVA, might be just the thing. Along the way, you'll stop on the sandy beaches of the Oxbow Preserve, the only riparian block on the river, and, if you ask Drew Dickson, he will tell you how his father wrote the original grant that created this natural preserve. At the end of your trip, you'll learn to shuck local Marin oysters from Tamales Bay, and Drew will pour you handcrafted wines from his family's Andrew Lane winery (page 169). Along the banks, you'll spot the wild grape vines that were the first hint to settlers that this was going to be a promising viticultural area.

Three-hour guided tours, with stand-up paddleboard lesson, oyster shucking, and wine pairing, starts at around $130. Independent paddleboard rentals start at $45 for a half-day for intrepid explorers.

Maps on pages viii–ix and x–xi

THE ST. HELENA HIGHWAY connects Napa and Calistoga and, running along the western side of the valley, is the region's main tasting route. Driving northward into the heart of Napa, you'll see billboard after billboard welcoming you to some of California's biggest and best-known wineries, places where tour buses and limousines roll in hourly and visitors can luxuriate in the splendor of vast gardens and gleaming tasting rooms. While the St. Helena Highway might not be exactly a back lane, along this familiar route there are dozens of small family wineries—off the highway and in the small towns of Yountville, Oakville, and Rutherford—that it would be easy to miss.

The wine country grew up around these kinds of places— family farms and old vineyards. Some have quietly been making wonderful small-production wines for the better part of a century. Others are old ghost wineries that have been reinvigorated by people who have come to the wine country more recently. Hidden in plain sight, these are some of the gems of the valley.

SHARON HARRIS FELL IN LOVE with wine during a junior year abroad at the University of Bordeaux when the wife of the university president invited the young college student to accompany her on a tour of the legendary estates at Château Haut-Brion. Sharon still laughs thinking of how that moment changed her life. In her mid-thirties, she returned to the University of Bordeaux to complete the prestigious DUAD wine program—the Diplôme Universitaire d'Aptitude à la Dégustation des Vins. And then she promptly moved to Napa. There, she founded an industry legend, the group Wine Entre Femmes, which led to groundbreaking collaborations between women winemakers in France and California.

Of course, Sharon also runs her own premium estate, Rarecat Wines, specializing in a luscious single-vineyard-designate Cabernet Sauvignon from the Old Hillside Toll Estate in Calistoga ($100) and in two whites—a cellar-worthy single-vineyard-designate Chardonnay from the famed Charles Heintz estates in Sonoma's Russian River AVA ($65) and a crisp and lightly floral Sauvignon Blanc from Napa Valley that is perfect for summer tasting ($30). Tasting at Rarecat is a private, hands-on experience with Sharon, and most of the spots go to members of her wine club and allocation list. But if you can't leave the valley without picking up some of these remarkable wines, there is a special request form on the Rarecat website. Check out the Rarecat social media sites, too. Sharon pours regularly at public tasting events nationally, maybe near you.

> ## RARECAT WINES
>
> P.O. Box 801, Rutherford
> Tasting off-site; call for details
>
> Tel. 650.464.9408,
> rarecatwines.com
>
> Tasting by appointment only

SET JUST BACK FROM Napa's main thoroughfare, Highway 29, Ehlers Estate is a historic winery with one of the valley's most unique stories. Founded by Jean Leducq, a wine enthusiast who was also heir to a French laundry fortune, Ehlers Estate could have been just another ultra-premium, high-profile winery. While it does fit that bill, the most amazing part of this family story is what Jean Leducq, who died from cardiac disease in 2002, did with that fortune. Today, Ehlers Estate is the asset of a medical trust, which funds university research into heart disease to the tune of $30 million annually. If the French paradox discovered that wine is good for the heart, then this is one winery helping to prove the point.

Ehlers also makes excellent wines, and, if you would like to add an educational component to your tasting experience in the Napa Valley, the winery offers some of the county's best programs. Visitors can register online for a visit that includes a tour of the organic vineyards and historic winery, followed by a sit-down tasting of their estate wines, which are paired with small plates. Ehlers has been making wines with a "green" approach since 2003.

If Ehlers is leading the way in sustainable viniculture in the wine country, this is also a place with deep historical roots in the valley. Another of Napa's ghost wineries, vineyards were first planted on this property in the nineteenth century by Bernard Ehlers, who built the stone winery that is still used as part of the production facility. In the summer, the courtyard just beyond is shaded by an orchard of olive trees that have stood for more

> ## EHLERS ESTATE
>
> **3222 Ehlers Lane
> Exit Ehlers Lane east from
> Highway 29**
>
> Tel. 707.963.5972,
> ehlersestate.com
>
> **Tasting daily 10:30 a.m. to
> 4:30 p.m.**

than a century, and the lush kitchen gardens are reminiscent of Jean Leducq's first foray into the winemaking business—when he purchased a vineyard in Virginia on land where Thomas Jefferson had once grown grapes and run a gentleman's farm.

The estate is comprised of thirty-nine acres planted to vine—mainly the Napa Valley's celebrated Cabernet Sauvignon, but Ehlers also produces a Merlot, Cabernet Franc, Petit Verdot, and one of the few St. Helena–appellated Sauvignon Blancs. The wines range from around $30 to $100, with most in the $50 range, and the annual production is around sixty-five hundred cases. Tasting fee is $25, and reservations are required only for parties of six or more.

ALBINO PESTONI left Italy for the Napa Valley back in 1882 and just a decade later founded the Bell Canyon Bonded Winery No. 935. The current Pestoni family ranchlands, though, date to the 1920s, when this valley was still covered with cattle and fruit orchards. Then, for years the lands were planted to vine, and the family sold the fruit to premium winemakers across the valley.

Today, Bob and Sylvia Pestoni are the proprietors of their own estate, the Rutherford Grove Winery, founded in the mid-1990s, and they are lucky enough to farm seventy acres of land and no fewer than ten estate vineyards in several different appellations. The result? Wines that represent all the richness of the area. While the primary focus is on Cabernet Sauvignon and Merlot varietals, there are also Sauvignon Blanc, Sangiovese, and Petite Sirah offerings. They also make a mountain Zinfandel with fruit from nearby Lake County, to the north of Napa. Wines range from around $20 to $65.

Estate and reserve tastings don't require an appointment ($15 to $25, waived with purchase), so this is a great choice if your wine country weekend is shaping up to be a spontaneous one, and the grounds are lovely. Picnics are welcome with the purchase of a bottle of wine or with a tasting, and you can also call ahead to reserve a food-and-wine pairing that they will organize for you. A rarity in the wine country, the tasting room is also pet friendly. And if you find yourself in the wine country without a place to stay, the Pestoni family runs the charming little Hotel d'Amici in downtown Calistoga (hoteldamici.com). The name means "friends' hotel" in Italian, and the Pestoni family takes that seriously.

TASTING AT Allora Vineyards takes place in the wine cellars built underneath the cheerful yellow stucco home surrounded by olive trees and vineyards that Terry and Nancy Klein purchased in the 1990s. Terry grew up here in the heart of the Napa Valley and made his name working in architectural plastering, but making wine had always been on his mind.

The land here had been recognized as ideal for growing grapes as early as the 1800s, but the Kleins first began growing grapes on the fifteen-acre property in the late 1990s. Their first vintage was only a hundred cases. Now there are ten acres of organically farmed vineyards, planted to Cabernet Sauvignon, Cabernet Franc, and Petite Sirah, and during the harvest the grapes are hand-picked and hand-sorted.

The winery, which takes its name from an Italian expression that roughly translates to "well, then," produces around twelve hundred cases of just over a half-dozen different wines: a reserve Cabernet Sauvignon, a Bordeaux blend, a Cabernet Franc, a Sauvignon-Blanc-led white, a Sangiovese and Cabernet blend, a Petite Sirah, and a late-harvest dessert wine made from a tantalizing blend of Cabernet and Petite Sirah (prices from $30 to $150). Here, the emphasis isn't on maximizing yields but on making a wine the family can be proud of, so during the growing season they "drop" almost half the fruit on the Cabernet vines—winemaker's lingo for the process of pruning a proportion of unripe fruit early in the season to ensure richly concentrated flavors and sugars in the grapes that remain come fall. The wines are barrel fermented and made with wild yeasts, and the minimal sulfites added the wines are organic, so wine enthusiasts prone to headaches are less likely to suffer for their pleasures.

The winemaker's tour and tasting is hosted by candlelight in the underground wine library. You'll want to ask Terry about his unique imported crystal stemware collection, with glasses that are modern adaptations of a traditional Italian design able to open the bouquet of a wine and a stylish decanter that is easy to clean (prices starting at $40). Afterward, you can stroll through the family's lush Tuscan-style gardens or take a peek at the vineyards just beyond. The fee for tasting ranges from $25 for a flight of four wines to $40 for the reserve tasting of library wines, and tasting fees are always waived for wine club members.

STONY HILL VINEYARD

3331 St. Helena Highway
(Highway 29)
Call for directions

Tel. 707.963.2636,
stonyhillvineyard.com

Tasting Monday to Friday by
appointment only

THE ROAD THAT LEADS UP to Stony Hill Vineyard is a single-lane track just before the entrance to the Bale Mill State Park, and here the moss hangs low from the oak and madrone trees before giving way at the crest of the hill to sweeping views of the Napa Valley. Among all the many charming wineries in the valley, Stony Hill is a standout. While tasting wine out in the summer tasting room—a patio table with the world at your feet—it is easy to find yourself entertaining thoughts of never going home.

Peter McCrea's father bought this 160-acre property in the 1940s and, in the years after the Second World War, planted it mostly to Chardonnay and to some German varietals using a tractor he bought secondhand from one of the local ranchers. He established Stony Hill Vineyard—bonded California winery No. 4461—in 1952, long before the winemaking renaissance that turned Napa Valley into a household name. In fact, this longevity makes Stony Hill one of the oldest wineries in the valley still owned by the same family. (The oldest is Krug, just down on the valley floor.)

Today, the estate winery is run by Peter and his wife, Willinda, and their daughter, Sarah. They make a unique style of wine that also happens to be one of the great bargains of the Napa Valley. The average production is around four thousand cases of wine a year, including a Chablis-style Chardonnay (around $40) made with no malolactic fermentation and in neutral oak barrels. "It's Chardonnay that tastes like Chardonnay," Peter will tell you. Winemaker Mike Chelini—who has been with Stony Hill for forty years and is only the second winemaker in the estate's history—also makes delicious drier-style Riesling and Gewürztraminer wines (in the $25 to $30 range) and a handcrafted Semillon dessert wine made from grapes originally found at France's legendary Château d'Yquem ($30). Stony Hill has also added a Cabernet to its repertoire ($60), and it's made in the historic style of mountain Cabernet rather than the fruit-forward style you'll find in much of the valley. At a modest 13.5 percent alcohol, it's food friendly and balanced.

The cost of for a tour is $25 per person, which they are happy to apply to wine purchases during your visit. The visit includes a leisurely walk to the winery, where Riesling is still made in fifty-year-old German barrels and where visitors can take a step back into California history to see what this valley must have been like in the beginning.

ELIZABETH SPENCER WINES
ELIZABETH SPENCER 0.0 m
1.0 mi HONIG
1.1 mi ROUND POND
Niebaum-Coppola's RUBICON ESTATE 0.3 mi
1.7 mi FROG'S LEAP
2.7 mi AUBERGE DU SOLEIL
2796 mi CHARLOTTESVILLE
2860 mi PHILADELPHIA
3084 mi

JUST A STONE'S THROW from the St. Helena Highway and tucked away in the small village of Rutherford is one of the wine country's most charming finds. The tasting room at Elizabeth Spencer Wines—the shared passion of Elizabeth Pressler and Spencer Graham—is the original brick post office of the village. Today, the 1872 building, covered in the summer months with a profusion of morning glory vines and jasmine, is a retreat for the senses.

ELIZABETH SPENCER

1165 Rutherford Road
East on Rutherford Road from
Highway 29

Tel. 707.963.6067,
elizabethspencerwines.com

Tasting daily 10 a.m. to
6 p.m.; cottage tastings by
appointment only

Elizabeth and Spencer met and married when she was launching her wine-marketing company in Napa and he was a chef and fine-wine distributor. Creating their own wines and brand seemed like a perfect way to celebrate their partnership, so, in 1998, they produced their first vintage and subsequently opened the Rutherford tasting room in 2006. Now, visitors gather around the cozy zinc bar or, during the summer months, head out to the enclosed garden just beyond the patio door. Flagship wines are the Cabernet Sauvignon offerings, but fans of Northern Californian Sauvignon Blanc, Chardonnay, Pinot Noir, and Syrah wines will also find something to delight ($40 to $75 range).

At Elizabeth Spencer, there are several unique tasting experiences on offer ($20 and up), with everything from a traditional tasting at the bar (no appointment needed but strongly recommended in summer) to an exploration of appellations (10:30 a.m. only), a chance to test your nose and try a blind tasting (1 p.m. and 3 p.m. only, weekdays), or even—for the real wine country aficionados—a casual wine country lunch with the owners (reservations required).

MACAULEY VINEYARDS first made
its reputation back in the 1980s as a
premium producer of late-harvest Sauvignon Blanc wines, when the winery
was founded by Ann Macauley Watson,
one of the first women to graduate from
Harvard with an M.B.A. and, back then,
one of the few women in the wine business as well. She bought nine acres of
vineyard property just south of the old bale mill on the St. Helena
Highway and planned a life in the wine country.

Her son, Mac, an avid wine collector whose passion for
fine vintages was ignited by a bottle of Château Lafite Roths-
child that he shared with his dad as a teenager, revived the family
label in 2001. From the start, the Macauley wines have received
striking accolades. Mac's 2004 Cabernet Sauvignon, made
by winemaker Kirk Venge, with fruit sourced from the legendary Beckstoffer To Kalon vineyard, was rated 96 points in *Wine
Spectator*; the 2005 To Kalon earned 91 points in *Wine Advocate* with Robert Parker's simple recommendation that "these
wines merit attention." There is also a small production of pep-
pery Zinfandel (wines from $35 to $150).

There are limited tasting appointments available ($45, cred-
ited toward purchase). The private winemaker's tour starts out
at the kitchen table of Mac's vineyard ranch home. The total production is eight hundred cases annually.

KEEVER VINEYARDS

26 Vineyard View Drive,
Yountville
Directions provided with
appointment

Tel. 707.944.0910,
keevervineyards.com

Tasting by appointment only

JUST OVER THE CREST of a hill on a small road in the western foothills of the Napa Valley is the early-California-style winery at Keever Vineyards, one of the area's newcomers. Run by the husband-and-wife team of Bill and Olga Keever, along with their son, Jason, and their daughter, Ashley, this two-generation family estate—a "retirement plan gone beautifully wrong"—opened to the public in 2006.

Bill graduated from Napa High School in 1963. His family had made its home in the valley for the better part of a decade, but Bill spent his working life in other parts of the state, later living abroad with Olga and their two children. He jokes that, when he and his wife retired to this twenty-one-acre vineyard property, the plan was to sell some grapes and spend their days playing golf. But hillside Cabernet Sauvignon is a prized commodity in the wine country, and their vineyard manager encouraged them to make some of their own wines.

Working with winemaker Celia Welch—*Food & Wine* magazine's winemaker of the year for 2008—Keever makes a small range of wines annually, including a signature estate 100 percent Cabernet Sauvignon ($95) made with fruit that has never left the property. The winery also produces a Bordeaux-style blend of Cabernet Sauvignon, Merlot, and Cabernet Franc, with small proportions of other Bordeaux varietals from time to time (around $70). They also produce a great fruity Sauvignon Blanc (under $35).

The spacious tasting room has views over the eastern hills of the valley, as far as Mount George and Atlas Peak, and there are deep leather armchairs where you can catch your breath if all that wine tasting is proving too exhausting. The tasting ($35) includes a tour of the family's vineyards, the state-of-the-art gravity-flow winery, and the hillside caves, which by some wonder of acoustics have a special whisper spot, which might just be the wine country's most unique spot for a wedding proposal. Visits are by appointment only.

BISTRO JEANTY

**6510 Washington Street,
Yountville
East on Washington Street
from Highway 29**

**Tel. 707.944.0103,
bistrojeanty.com**

**Open Monday to Sunday
11:30 a.m. to 10:30 p.m.**

THE FRENCH know how to do bistro dining like no one else—understated elegance and excellent food served up with a sense of community spirit and a warm welcome—and if I were to choose a favorite spot in the Napa Valley to settle in for a long lunch or a romantic dinner in the Parisian style, it would be Bistro Jeanty. Owner and chef Philippe Jeanty hails from the Champagne region of France and first came to the wine country in the 1970s as part of the team sent over to open the signature restaurant at Domaine Chandon. He opened the doors to his own bistro in 1998, and it was immediately recognized as one of the best new restaurants in the Bay Area.

Set just along the main street in the picturesque little town of Yountville, where you can while away an afternoon in the local antique shops and the nearby shopping gallery, Bistro Jeanty can be recognized by the brightly colored flowers pouring out of the window boxes and the candy-stripe red-and-white awning that sets the cheerful and intimate tone. Signature dishes include escargots served with pastis butter, home-smoked trout salad, a fabulous coq au vin, and, for those who like their beef blue, steak tartare with frites. Most entrées are priced at $20 to $25, and corkage is a reasonable $15.

A HIGH-END LOCAL favorite, Redd, chef Richard Reddington's wine country restaurant, is an oasis of contemporary modernist décor. If you're looking for an elegant evening out and willing to splurge a bit on some formally presented cuisine, this is where the valley's winemakers and entrepreneurs come for great food in the new California style. The food is consistently excellent. Entrées run around $30, and at $25 the corkage fee is a bit on the expensive side. But there is an expansive local wine list, and this is a place where you can try wines you won't find anywhere else.

REDD

6480 Washington Street, Yountville
East on Washington Street from Highway 29

Tel. 707.944.2222, reddnapavalley.com

Open daily 11:30 a.m. to 2:30 p.m., 5:30 p.m. to 9:30 p.m.

BALE GRIST MILL STATE HISTORIC PARK AND BOTHE-NAPA VALLEY STATE PARK

3369 St. Helena Highway
Just south of the Ehlers Lane
intersection

Tel. 707.942.4575,
napavalleystateparks.org

Closed major holidays;
overnight camping requires
a permit

DURING THE LATTER PART of the nineteenth century, Napa Valley farmers didn't rely on the production of grapes. In those pioneer days, wheat led the local economy. So when Edward Turner Bale—a physician working for General Vallejo—settled down to make a home for himself in St. Helena in 1846, he built the water-powered gristmill that quickly became the center of public life in the valley.

The mill continued to operate until the early decades of the twentieth century, and it has since been converted into a state historic park where visitors can tour the site. On weekends, there are often milling demonstrations, where you can purchase bags of freshly ground cornmeal polenta. Nearby is the site of Napa's first church and the original nineteenth-century community cemetery.

Adjacent to the Bale Grist Mill State Historic Park is the nearly two-thousand-acre Bothe-Napa Valley State Park (pronounced bow-thay), which offers year-round camping and hiking on a variety of trails, where you can stroll through redwood groves, visit the Native American garden, or dip your toes in the creek. For those looking for unique lodging in the wine country, the park also boasts a small number of yurts—permanent tents that come with a queen-size bed and a private fire pit ($60 to $75 a night; maximum of six occupants).

There is no charge to enter the Bale Historic Park, but there is a small fee for the mill tours; the Bothe-Napa Valley State Park charges a modest day-use fee. The gristmill is in operation when you see the "Milling Today" sign at the park entrance. Keep in mind that with budget cuts in California in recent years, state park opening times, fees, and public access often change quickly; be sure to check their website when planning for the most current information.

IF YOU THINK the mountain views from your favorite back lane winery are spectacular, imagine what it's like flying over the Napa Valley at dawn in a hot air balloon. After landing, it's a field-side Champagne breakfast at Domaine Chandon, one of Napa's premiere producers of sparkling wines. It just might be the quintessential wine country experience. Needless to say, if you're planning a wedding, honeymoon, or (gentlemen: a hint) romantic proposal, there are few more memorable ways to do it than from a thousand feet above vineyards at first light.

There are several professional balloon companies in the county, and one of the oldest and most renowned is Napa Valley Balloons, which is consistently voted the best balloon ride in the county. Balloons can accommodate up to ten people, and rates per person start at around $215 (winter and website discounts often available). Reservations need to be made at least twenty-four hours in advance, and during the summer several weeks in advance is recommended. Balloons lift off at sunrise, and flight time is one hour.

THE IDEA OF CYCLING in the warm California sunshine past the vineyards when the mustard fields are in bloom is decidedly romantic. If you are planning to spend your days tasting wines without the aid of dump buckets, it's also decidedly practical. Along the back lanes, coasting from one winery to the next, it's never a bad idea to gather one's wits with a small roadside picnic or perhaps even the briefest of naps.

Of course, you can make a serious endeavor of all this biking as well, if you like. The country roads in the wine country are among the world's most beautiful.

Whatever your pleasure, whether it's a bike tour or just an afternoon rental you're after, one of the friendliest spots to find two wheels is the Napa Valley Bike Tours company. The staff will happily advise you on some of the area's most scenic routes, and full-day rentals start at around $40, tandems at around $80. Free roadside assistance is included, and they also rent tag-alongs and trailers if you're traveling the wine country with younger children. With a bit of advance planning, wine country connoisseurs can map out a series of unique tasting appointments and have purchases mailed home.

If advance planning is not your thing, you can leave it to the folks at Napa Valley Bike. They offer guided tours (either as part of a group or with a private guide; starting at around $140) that include a picnic lunch, pickup and delivery of your wines, and scheduled tasting appointments with nearby local vintners.

Maps on pages viii–ix

WHILE HOWELL MOUNTAIN was the first recognized subappellation in the Napa Valley and remains the most widely known eastern hillside AVA in the wine country, there are several wonderful small wineries tucked away in the mountains rising above the valley floor. Some of these wineries are located in distinct subappellations like the Chiles Valley AVA or the Pope Valley AVA, where unique microclimates and growing conditions help create wines with a very particular character and expression of terroir. Other areas in these sometimes remote and wild valleys are simply part of the prestigious Napa Valley AVA, although areas like Pritchard Hill are well known to devoted wine aficionados.

The drive up to these wineries takes you along country roads, often through miles of undeveloped valley terrain, and you won't find any of those charming bistros back here. There aren't many gasoline stations, either. If what you are looking for is an experience of the landscape at its most beautifully bucolic and a chance to sample some wines that are unlike what you'll find down on the valley floor, then these eastern hillside vineyards offer new discoveries.

THE NICHELINI FAMILY has been making wines here in the eastern hills of Napa County since the 1890s, and their vintage farmhouse and tasting room might just be one of the most charming rustic little places you'll encounter out here as you head into the Chiles Valley. The family will tell you that they are the oldest continually operating winery in the Napa Valley, and a visit to them is a chance to step back into history and get a glimpse of what the wine country must have been like just a couple of generations ago.

NICHELINI FAMILY WINERY

2950 Sage Canyon Road,
St. Helena
East on Sage Canyon Road
from Highway 121

Tel 707.963.0717,
nicheliniwinery.com

Tasting Friday, Saturday, and
Sunday 10 a.m. to 5 p.m.,
other days by appointment

Nichilini specializes in making wines from fruit grown on family property in the Chiles Valley, including a Chardonnay and a delicious Sauvignon Vert—made from the white Bordeaux Muscadelle grape. There are also several red wines, ranging from the classic Cabernet Sauvignon and Merlot varietals to a port-style dessert wine and a Primitivo that recently took home a medal in the San Francisco International Wine Competition. Winemaker Aimée Sunseri is the fifth generation in her family to take the helm and a graduate of the wine program at the University of California Davis. Most wines are around $30, and there is no charge for tasting.

VOLKER EISELE FAMILY ESTATE

3080 Lower Chiles Valley
Road, St. Helena
East on Sage Canyon Road
from Highway 121, north
on Chiles Pope Valley Road,
south on Lower Chiles
Valley Road

Tel. 707.965.9485,
volkereiselefamilyestate.com

Tasting by appointment only

ABOUT FIFTEEN MINUTES east of St. Helena, on a small winding back lane, you'll come across the old wooden winery that is home to the Volker Eisele Family Estate. The building was constructed in the 1870s, and, with its weathered tin roof and bleached exterior, there is something essentially Northern Californian about it all. Old fir floor planks creak pleasantly, and on a hot summer day in the Napa Valley—because days can get hot in the wine country—it's worth remembering that things stay a bit cooler up here at twelve hundred feet.

Chiles Valley, an arm of the Napa Valley, is long and narrow, running from northwest to southeast, and the small family wineries in this region are making some of Napa County's most interesting new wines. Even if Chiles Valley is just gaining widespread recognition as one of Napa's premium appellations, people have been quietly making excellent Cabernet wines out here for generations. Volker and Liesel Eisele have been growing grapes in their sixty-acre vineyard since the mid-1970s, and today, along with their son Alexander, they release a small production of estate wines made with Bordeaux varietals. Replanting has all been done in the original footprint of the 1870s vineyard, and the vineyards are certified organic.

Volker and Liesel met while studying at the University of California, both having come to the Bay Area from Germany. Curiously enough, few people know that there is a long tradition of German immigrants shaping winemaking in the Napa Valley, despite the fact that at the end of the nineteenth and the beginning of the twentieth century German families were a major presence in the wine country.

The Eisele family started out as growers and didn't release their first commercial vintage until the early 1990s. They now produce four different wines: Gemini, a crisp, white blend of Semillon and Sauvignon Blanc that *Wine Enthusiast* recently gave 93 points and called "one of the best wines of its type"; a beautifully complex Cabernet Sauvignon; their signature cofermented Terzetto blend, made with Cabernet Sauvignon, Cabernet Franc, and Merlot (ranging from $25 to $75); and a special reserve Alexander Cabernet Sauvignon—a minute production of just six barrels—sold only from the tasting room and in boxes of three ($375). The fee for tasting is $35.

RUSTRIDGE BED AND BREAKFAST AND WINERY

2910 Lower Chiles Valley
Road, St. Helena
East on Sage Canyon Road
from Highway 121, north
on Chiles Pope Valley Road,
south on Lower Chiles
Valley Road

Tel. 707.965.9353,
rustridge.com

Tasting daily at 11 a.m.,
1 p.m., and 3 p.m. by
appointment only

IF YOU ARE LONGING TO GET AWAY for a wine country weekend but the fancy spas up in Calistoga aren't your cup of tea, the RustRidge Winery—which does double duty as a bed-and-breakfast and as a working ranch and horse farm—is the kind of place where you can fall off the grid for a few days of real peace and quiet. During harvest, guests can watch the crush firsthand, and that's the kind of education in the life of a wine-maker you won't find many places. If you visit during the other eleven months of the year, there are gourmet breakfasts, hiking trails, tennis courts, and even an on-site sauna to enjoy.

When you're not out wine tasting, of course. And wine tasting at RustRidge can begin right after a hearty breakfast. It's a great opportunity to discover the Chiles Valley, one of Napa's less familiar but most distinctive appellations. The valley is known for its production of Claret-style Zinfandel wines; RustRidge is also known for its Chardonnay. The grape develops beautifully here at this elevation, where the nights can get cold even in the summer months.

The husband-and-wife team of Susan Meyer and Jim Fresquez run the ranch, which Susan's parents bought in the 1970s. Her father and brothers planted the first vineyards on the property in 1975. Now Jim and Susan, with partner Kent Rosenblum, make seven different wines: the signature Zinfandel and Chardonnay wines; the highly acclaimed red and white blends, called (in a nod to the more than fifteen horses they keep in the stables) Racehorse Red and Racehorse White; a Sauvignon Blanc; a Chardonnay; a Cabernet Sauvignon; and a Zinfandel. The Chardonnay and Racehorse Red have taken gold medals in the *San Francisco Chronicle* wine competition in recent years. Total case production is around three thousand, and the well-priced wines range from $25 to $50. The standard tasting fee is $20, and the reserve Cabernet tasting is $30. Room rates, if you are hoping to take in the full RustRidge experience, are in the $165 to $350 range.

TUCKED FAR UP INTO the hills to the east of the valley floor, Amizetta (pronounced ahm-ah-zet-uh) is well off the beaten path. It would be a shame to miss either the beauty of this pastoral retreat or this special little winery run by the husband-and-wife team of Spencer and Amizetta Clark—the latter a fifteenth-generation direct descendent of Pocahontas.

Back in the 1970s when they purchased the property, Napa wasn't yet known for its hillside vineyards. They planted the land to grapes themselves in the early 1980s, intending to sell the fruit to some of the high-end wineries cropping up in the valley. Before long, of course, they were producing their own wines, and they released their first Cabernet Sauvignon in 1985. Today the winery produces around thirty-five hundred cases a year, focusing on Cabernet Sauvignon and red Bordeaux varietals, including a Cabernet Sauvignon, Merlot, and Cabernet Franc blend called Complexity. They also produce a Merlot and an old-vine "Vignetto" reserve Cabernet, which was recently a double gold medal winner at the San Francisco Wine competition.

Tasting takes place amid the sweet smells of oak barrels at an old pine table in the cave, where the year-round temperature is an ideal sixty-three degrees and where the soothing sounds of a bubbling spring weren't part of any grand plan—they discovered it when excavating. Tours are by appointment only. The tasting fee is $25, waived with purchase. The wines run from around $35 to $85.

WINE TASTING at Heibel Ranch Vineyards with proprietor Trent Ghiringhelli is up on the mountaintop with long views of the Pope Valley. Sitting here above the fog line, sipping some wine and taking it all in, is what the back lane experience is all about.

Visitors to these ranch vineyards—owned and operated by Trent; his mother, Helen; and stepfather, Bruce Nelson—travel more than a mile off the county road, through ancient stands of redwood trees and along ridges with gnarled manzanita, as part of the winemaker's tour. This 186-acre hillside property is the parcel of land the family retained when they sold the Aetna Springs Resort, long a favorite haunt of old Hollywood and a piece of California history. Here, Ronald Reagan announced his first run for the governorship in the 1960s.

Heibel Ranch—the name is a nod to Helen's father, George Bennett Heibel, who purchased Aetna Springs Resort back in 1945—released its first vintage in 2006, and the wine sold out in a matter of months. The estate produces a proprietary Napa Valley red blend called Lappa's ($40), made with Cabernet Sauvignon, Zinfandel, and a bit of Petite Sirah. It's grown on their two-acre, certified organic, estate vineyard that the family cleared on weekends and now farms by hand. They have recently added a Cabernet Sauvignon (around $75) and a Zinfandel dessert wine in the port style ($35). The tasting fee is $35.

HEIBEL RANCH VINEYARDS

1241 Adams Street, Suite 1043, St. Helena
Tasting off-site; call or email for directions

Tel. 707.968.9289,
hrvwines.com

Tours by appointment only

CHAPTER 9
LOS CARNEROS AND ENVIRONS SOUTH OF NAPA

WINERIES

PROVISIONS

Maps on pages xii–xiii

WITH ONE FOOT IN SONOMA COUNTY and the other foot in Napa, the southern AVA known as Los Carneros—named after the nearby Carneros Creek and meaning "the rams" in Spanish—is cooled on hot summer days by the fog that rolls in from San Pablo Bay. The result is a cool-climate terroir at the southern tip of the wine country, an area famous for its Pinot Noir, Chardonnay, and sparkling wines. With easy access to both downtown Napa and the historic plaza in the city of Sonoma, there are plenty of options to combine sightseeing and good food with tasting at some of the region's most accessible and interesting small wineries.

BOURASSA VINEYARDS

190 Camino Oruga, Napa
North on Kelly Road from
Highway 12, south on
Camino Dorado, southeast
on Camino Oruga

Tel. 707.254.4922,
bourassavineyards.com

Tasting Monday to Saturday
10 a.m. to 4 p.m.
by appointment only

THE TASTING ROOM at Bourassa Vineyards is in a commercial park off Highway 29, south of the city of Napa, and it might not fit the image of the rustic wine country that first comes to mind. But this is small-production winemaking at its most authentic, and it would be a mistake to miss a visit to what might just be one of the most intimate and inviting tasting rooms in the valley. Here, visitors sip wine in a candlelit tasting room, amid silver dump buckets and gleaming candelabra, and the feeling is surprisingly opulent and old-world. At Bourassa, the watchword is celebration, and it shows.

This small winery is the second-life dream of Vic Bourassa, who grew up in a French-Canadian family in New England and made his first career in real estate in Southern California. In the 1990s he came to Napa, and from there it is the familiar story: he fell in love with the lifestyle and with the modest idea of making a little bit of wine. He started out working in some Napa Valley tasting rooms, took a few classes, and eventually went on to become president of the Napa Valley Home Winemakers Association.

One afternoon, talking with his friend, the legendary winemaker Robert Mondavi, he brought out some of his homemade Pinot Noir, and a delighted Mondavi polished off the bottle. Despite making an excellent wine, Vic worried that it was too late to start a second career at fifty. He tells the story of how Mondavi reminded him that he didn't get his start in wine until he was fifty-five, and that turned out pretty well. So in 2001, Vic released his first vintage—four hundred cases of wine.

Today, thanks to the strong reputation of his wines, Bourassa Vineyards produces around five thousand cases. The winery is best known for its Bordeaux blends and for working with some unusual varietals, including Petit Verdot, although visitors will find everything from a crisp Sauvignon Blanc to a port-style dessert wine on offer.

Most tastings range from $20 to $35 and include some of the essentials of wine education, tailored to your level of experience. This is a place where beginners can learn about the importance of oak in winemaking or how to distinguish different varietals; more experienced or adventurous aficionados might want to reserve one of the special blending seminars ($50), where you'll construct your own Bordeaux blend in a glass. Set aside some extra time if you want to take a morning tour that includes a visit to the Seguin Moreau cooperage (seguinmoreau napa.com) just down the lane, a fascinating, firsthand education in the traditional art of making barrels.

If you can't make it to Bourassa Vineyards on this trip, here's something else to consider: a winemaker's tasting party in your home. Vic travels widely and loves to share his passion for great wines.

MCKENZIE-MUELLER

2530 Las Amigas Road, Napa
South on Cuttings Wharf Road
from Highway 121, southwest
on Las Amigas Road

Tel. 707.252.0186,
mckenziemueller.com

Tasting by appointment only

THERE ARE FEW PLACES in the wine country where you'll feel more at home than in the barn-style tasting room at McKenzie-Mueller. This working winery and ranch is tucked away on a residential back road where it's easy to forget, even at the height of the summer tourist season, the more than five million visitors who make their way to Napa's wine country every year. There's none of the glitz and hustle up here—just vineyards and farms and maybe a bit of a breeze coming in off San Pablo Bay.

Of course, there are friendly folks and some new wines to discover, too. For a small family operation, making just three thousand cases of wine a year, McKenzie-Mueller produces an impressive range. Son Julius likes to joke that his parents are so committed to trying a little bit of everything that he even has two middle names. If you're on the tasting trail with someone who can't quite decide on a favorite style, here's the chance to do some serious sampling: you'll find everything from Chardonnay and Merlot to Cabernet Franc, Cabernet Sauvignon, and Malbec (most wines $20 to $45). There is a lovely Sauvignon Blanc that might just be the perfect thing for a summer afternoon in a shady hammock, and, of course, they serve up the Carneros signature wines—beautiful Pinot Noirs.

The McKenzie and Mueller families have roots here that go back generations. Bob's family settled in Napa in the late 1800s and owned vineyards up in Rutherford, but he likes to say that he really learned the craft during his fifteen-year stint as a winemaker over at the University of Mondavi—an affectionate local reference to the generous professional development and entrepreneurial encouragement that Robert Mondavi offered his employees.

Karen and Bob purchased their first ten acres of vineyards in the late 1970s, and a decade later they bought their current property on Las Amigas Road. By the early 1990s, they went into winemaking on their own, full time. Today it's a second-generation family enterprise, and both daughter Sam and son Julius share the passion for growing grapes and the craft of viniculture. They've also recently started producing olive oil from trees on the farm. All the wines at McKenzie-Mueller are made from estate fruit and are bottled unfiltered. Although these are wines that have won a raft of gold and double gold medals from wine competitions, the emphasis here is on learning to trust your own palate and on finding a wine you'll enjoy. Bob insists that everyone who tastes wine has the ability to make smart judgments, and there's always a standing invitation to come out to their tasting room and give it a try. The $10 tasting fee is waived with purchase, unless you are coming as part of a large group.

CHRIS AND NAOMI THORPE bought this thirty-three-acre ranch in the Carneros back in the 1980s, and their first thought was to raise cattle. But the cattle kept wandering, and Chris likes to joke that he blames his neighbor for getting him into the wine business. The neighbor was clearing his property to put in vineyards and offered to let Chris use the machinery. So in 1990, the family planted their first eight acres, and later another twelve. Today the vineyards are planted to Chardonnay, Merlot, Pinot Noir, and Syrah along the northeast slopes, and the family has returned this pre-Prohibition estate to vineyards for the first time in generations.

Known to settlers in the nineteenth century as Rancho Huichica—which translates from the hybridization of Spanish and native Wappo languages as "Owl Ranch"—this property has a long history in the wine country. The first white settlers here were a Danish family in the early 1800s who bought forty acres for a thousand dollars in gold coins as part of a Mexican land grant. The historic ranch still has an old pioneer-style outhouse down at the far end of the lawn. During a recent renovation, Chris discovered an old root and wine cellar under the floorboards in the farmhouse—complete with hundred-year-old empty beer bottles. Owls still live in the nineteenth-century barn that serves as the Adastra tasting room.

Chris is an astronomy enthusiast, and the name Adastra comes from the Latin motto *per aspera ad astra*—"through hard work to the stars." Part of that work, of course, is running the winery, which produces fewer than fifteen hundred cases of 100 percent estate wines (most $40 to $60). All the grapes are grown organically. Situated just a few miles from San Pablo Bay, the vineyards are perfect for cooler-climate grapes like Pinot Noir and Chardonnay. The 2005 Syrah was awarded an impressive 93 points by *Wine Spectator*. Son-in-law Edwin started making a few bottles of a Californian table wine under a second label—Ed's Red—a couple of years back, and since then the wine has become a big favorite as far away as Hong Kong. Today they make more than two thousand cases of Ed's Red in addition to the Adastra offerings ($15; edsred.net).

Tasting with the winegrower includes a tour of the historic family property and is around $25; one tasting fee is waived for every $150 in purchases.

TRUCHARD VINEYARDS

3234 Old Sonoma Road, Napa
Call for directions

Tel. 707.253.7153,
truchardvineyards.com

Tasting daily by appointment
only; closed Sunday

SOMETIMES LIFE in the wine country begins in the most unusual way, and, if you start asking the county's winemakers how they got their start, you'll hear stories of honeymoon weekends or lucky invitations or chance encounters. The story that Jo Ann and Tony Truchard tell might just be the most fateful of all because, as they explain, it all began with Jo Ann slipping on a grape in 1972.

Back then, Tony was an Army doctor who had just received orders to Korea when his wife slipped on a grape in the local grocery store and broke her knee. Four days later, the couple's son was born, and, instead of going to Korea, the family ended up on the Army base in Herlong, California.

That autumn, they visited Napa. Tony had grown up on a ranch in Texas, where his French grandfather had tended a small vineyard on the property for years. Enchanted by Napa, they started looking for a piece of property and ended up finding the perfect spot—a twenty-one-acre parcel in the Carneros region, planted to pastures and prune orchards, which they visited on weekends. They converted the property to vineyards and sold their grapes to the Carneros Creek Winery. Then, in 1987, Tony bought a local medical practice, and the couple moved to Napa full time. Two years later, Truchard Vineyards released its first commercial vintage, specializing in Pinot Noir and Chardonnay—the signature varietals of this southern subappellation.

Today, the couple farms around 270 acres of their four-hundred-acre property, making around a dozen different wines from ten different varietals (from $20 to $75, most around $35). By Napa Valley standards, this is a huge piece of property, but, as they will tell you, they are a large vineyard and a small winery—producing just over fifteen thousand cases of wine and selling the majority of their fruit to more than twenty recognized winemakers in the region.

While they still make some of the signature Carneros Pinot Noir and Chardonnay, excellent Cabernet Sauvignon, Petit Verdot, Cabernet Franc, and Merlot wines are also produced at Truchard. As one of the warmest vineyards in the appellation, they are able to get great fruit from some of the traditional Bordeaux varietals—and from spicier fruits like Syrah, Zinfandel, and Tempranillo. In addition to the Chardonnay, there is a small Roussanne program. The *San Francisco Chronicle* named the winery's 2006 Roussanne one of the top 100 wines of the year—and at $20 a bottle it's one of the valley's best deals. You'll also find a late-harvest dessert wine made from Roussanne, and if you aren't familiar with either this Rhône varietal or with the magic of botrytis, the noble rot, Truchard is a great place to discover something new.

All the wines are 100 percent grown, bottled, and produced on the estate. The emphasis is on wines that one crafted without a lot of manipulation, that age well, and that are easy to enjoy with food. Tastings take place in a rustic redwood barn next door to the family's farmhouse, and the visit includes a tour of the caves. The path up to the vineyards is lined with roses that come tumbling out in all directions. Here at Truchard, where there are many different varietals on the property, the harvest goes on sometimes as long as ten weeks, and the fruit is still hand-harvested. You are welcome to come for a visit during the crush. There is no charge for a tasting unless you are part of a large group.

BOONFLY CAFÉ

4048 Sonoma Highway, Napa
Highway 121 west of
the Cuttings Wharf Road
intersection

Tel. 707.299.4900,
thecarnerosinn.com

Open daily 7 a.m. to 9 p.m.;
reservations for dinner only

DRIVING THROUGH Napa and Sonoma you can see some of the old barns and weather-washed water towers that are the vestiges of those old farming days in Northern California, and back in the mid-1800s one of those young pioneers in the Carneros was a man named Boon Fly. He planted some of the area's first orchards and vineyards.

Today, the roadhouse bistro at the celebrated Carneros Inn is named after that intrepid farmer, and if you're looking for a place to stop in the area, this is a great spot for lunch, dinner, or—especially—breakfast. The breakfast at the Boonfly Café, in fact, is widely regarded among locals as the best breakfast in Napa. Here, there is everything from homemade doughnuts and a California-style breakfast burrito to eggs benedict and a mean Bloody Mary. Breakfast will run you from $7 to $20, depending on your appetite, and brunch is just a bit higher. The Boonfly Café is also open daily for lunch and dinner, and the food is consistently delicious at other times of the day also.

Wine Shipping Services

UPS

36 Second Street, Napa

Tel. 707.265.6011 • theupsstore.com

Open Monday to Friday 8:30 a.m. to 6:30 p.m.,
Saturday 9 a.m. to 5 p.m., Sunday 10 a.m. to 2 p.m.

This little outlet in downtown Napa specializes in helping visitors get their wines home safely and economically, and I know of more than a few small wineries who use their services. The last time I needed to get a case of wine to New England, the young woman behind the counter kindly helped me figure out how to fit all those oddly shaped bottles of sparkling wine into the sturdy cardboard boxes that they provide, taped it up for me, and, for less than $80—a price that included the shipping and packaging—my precious cargo was on its way east. The services are well priced and convenient, and the staff is friendly.

NAPA VALLEY WINE STORAGE

1135 Golden Gate Drive, Napa
From St. Helena Highway (Highway 29)
Exit West Imola Avenue west to Golden Gate Drive south

Tel. 707.265.9990 • napavalleywinestorage.com

Many of the wine country's most serious collectors rely on Napa Valley Wine Storage, which offers high-end temperature- and humidity-controlled storage facilities. They also offer a range of shipping services. They will pick up from local wineries in both Napa and Sonoma counties, or you can arrange to drop off cases before heading out of town. If you're ending your tasting adventures along Highway 12/121, en route back to the Oakland or San Francisco airports, Napa Valley Wine Storage is an easy stop.

STAGE COACH EXPRESS AND COMPANY

3379 Solano Avenue, Napa
Solano Avenue, just south of Redwood Road/Trancas Street

Tel. 707.257.1888 • stagecoachexpress.com

One of the favorite shipping companies among the small family vintners, Stage Coach Express can help find a way to get your new collection back home, even if you live in a state where bottles can't be shipped directly from the winery. Proprietors Sue Bailey and Larry Rupp can arrange to pick up wines from local hotels or from the wineries, which is especially handy if you are thinking of joining wine clubs or buying futures to take advantage of the often significant discounts. Keep in mind that the company doesn't insure for temperature damage, so spring and autumn wine tasting trips are often more economical times of the year for shipping. Prices for delivering a case of wine start at around $70.

LALA WINES

lalawines.com

Over a dinner in Paris, a French friend once bemoaned the impossibility of traveling with more than a bottle or two of Californian fine wine, and many visitors to the wine country are from outside the United States. Out of compassion for our European friends (and there are many who come to the wine country) and find themselves stymied by all the customs-related complications of getting wines back home, some friends in New York City founded Lala Wines, an export company that specializes in delivering cases of those yummy small-lot California Cabernets (and any other varietal you fancy) back to the European Union at an affordable price via climate-controlled sea shipments and customs clearances. As one of the founders, I'm not precisely objective, but Lala Wines has a lot of fans among the world's more far-flung wine lovers.

About the Author & Photographer

TILAR J. MAZZEO is the Clara C. Piper Associate Professor of English at Colby College and the bestselling author of books on wine, luxury, and French history, including *The Widow Clicquot*, *The Secret of Chanel No. 5*, *The Back Lane Wineries of Sonoma*, *The Hotel on the Place Vendôme*, and the forthcoming *Irena's Children*. She divides her time between California wine country, Maine, and British Columbia.

PAUL HAWLEY is a wine-country native, raised on his family's vineyard in Sonoma's Dry Creek Valley. He graduated from the University of California, Santa Cruz, in 2003 with a degree in film production. His feature film, *Corked*, debuted in 2008. Most days he can be found behind his lens or at his family's Hawley winery.

Index

MORE WINE GUIDES
FROM TILAR MAZZEO

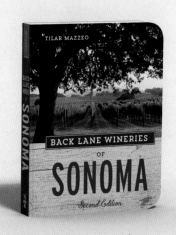

BACK LANE WINERIES OF SONOMA
$19.99 (Can $23.99)
ISBN: 978-1-60774-592-1
eBook ISBN: 978-1-60774-593-8